screencraft

directing

Mike Goodridge

screencraft

directing

RotoVision

A RotoVision Book

Published and distributed by RotoVision SA

Rue du Bugnon 7

CH-1299 Crans-Près-Céligny

Switzerland

RotoVision SA, Sales & Production Office

Sheridan House, 112/116A Western Road

Hove, East Sussex BN3 1DD, UK

Tel: +44 (0)1273 727 268

Fax: +44 (0)1273 727 269

E-mail: sales@rotovision.com

Website: www.rotovision.com

ISBN 2-88046-505-2

10 9 8 7 6 5 4 3 2 1

Design Copyright © 1998 Morla Design, Inc., San Francisco

Layout by Artmedia, London

Production and separation by ProVision Pte. Ltd., Singapore

Tel: +65 334 7720

Fax: +65 334 7721

contents

introduction

Ask a movie journalist about what sells – an interview with a film actor or an interview with a director – and he'll say actor just about every time. In today's celebrity-obsessed culture, actors have become more than just the marketing tools around which a film is sold to audiences. They have unwittingly become the spokespeople for the movies in which they appear, even though they probably haven't worked on the project itself for months. Disturbingly, the director, who has his or her stamp on the film before, during and after shooting, has been sidelined in the public perception. A director certainly doesn't make great copy like a movie star does, especially if that star has recently separated from a partner or been caught in a lewd act. But of course, behind the scenes and away from tabloid perceptions, the directors are the real stars of cinema. In a colourful quote made in early 2000, Ridley Scott said what many less outspoken film-makers just keep to themselves: "When actors say, 'what about my performance?', I say, 'what about my performance?' I'm responsible for the way it looks, the way it sounds, the way it's cast, what the locations look like, what the script's like, how the shoes are tied and how your hair is done. So back off and give me a little bit of space to coordinate these things – at which I'm maybe one of the best. I say it's not just about you. Ultimately, it's about me." The 'Directing' entry in the SCREENCRAFT series is all about them. 15 of the world's most celebrated living film-makers offer insight into the way they work, although, unlike previous subjects in the series, a director's job encompasses all the crafts, if not in execution, then in guidance, as well as shaping the script and instruction of the actors. A director dictates the mood and pace of the film, builds suspense, elicits comedy or generates emotion. Read Pedro Almodóvar's chapter, for example, to see how some directors sweat over every facial expression, every colour, every movement on film.

A word about the selection procedure. When I was commissioned to write the book, I drew up a shortlist of directors who would qualify for in-depth investigation into their body of work. My initial line-up came to 71. Whittling that down to 15 was a painful process of elimination based

around the selection criteria of different cultures and nationalities as well as distinct styles and pioneering achievements. Of course the choices are subjective, and some directors I would have loved to be included were not available, like Jean-Luc Godard, Ingmar Bergman, Billy Wilder, Eric Rohmer, Woody Allen or Claude Chabrol. Others, like Martin Scorsese and Zhang Yimou, were shooting and literally unreachable.

I visited most of the film-makers on their home territory and fortunately didn't have to conduct any interviews during promotional periods for specific films. That way, I believe they were more open and less jaded. Sitting drinking tea with Lars von Trier in his home in a suburb of Copenhagen, watching as Roman Polanski munched a cigar in his Paris office or as Milos Forman did likewise in the sitting room of his Connecticut house, the same room where he and Peter Shaffer laboured over the script and score for **Amadeus**, I had a sense that they were talking with clarity and candour about their work. The time span of a year over which I travelled to meet them afforded me the chance to catch them in that rare relaxed phase when they were in-between films. It was exhilarating, for example, to visit Mike Leigh in his London studios – beneath the "offices" of two working prostitutes, he gleefully told me – on a sofa on which only

weeks later he would be inviting actors to sit and meet for his next untitled film. Each interview was a surprise in that no two had the same things to say about the way they work. These 14 men and one woman have wildly differing inspirations, experiences, styles, approaches and disciplines. All, naturally, are larger-than-life, idiosyncratic personalities. That each had a different approach to film-making confirmed that, for this extraordinarily demanding and intensely personal job, no technique can be learned. Film school may teach a budding director about a wide-angle lens, but you cannot learn how to become Ken Loach or David Lynch. This book intends therefore only to offer insight into how unique talents such as these have evolved and how they put a film together from first idea to final cut. With such singularity at work, it's no surprise that some of the film-makers in the book have developed their own unmistakable brands. It's easy to recognise a film by Almodóvar or Oliver Stone just because of the signposts familiar from their body of work – the vivid colours and grand passions of the former, the fast, in-your-face cutting and operatic stylings of the latter. David Lynch has even spawned his own adjective "Lynchian", while James Ivory and his producing partner Ismail Merchant have become lodged in the world's consciousness simply as Merchant Ivory. Others strive to be more unobtrusive, happy to embrace a diverse range of styles according to the needs of

each story. Steven Soderbergh, for example, says he doesn't worry about imitators because he doesn't have an easily identifiable aesthetic, unlike Robert Altman, Scorsese or Lynch. Similarly, how can you define Ang Lee who is as accomplished directing a film of a Jane Austen novel as an American Civil War epic or a Mandarin martial-arts movie?

Some always write and direct – Takeshi Kitano, Almodóvar, Leigh, Lynch – others work with writers. Some religiously shoot in sequence – Leigh and Loach obviously, and Kitano, who usually also plays his own lead character – others can't afford that luxury or don't require it. All have one striking objective in common, which is the quest to put on screen a story, situations and characters which are truthful and true-to-life. Even David Lynch, who often jettisons linear narrative, is passionate about remaining true to the story. (What's more, when he does tell a traditional narrative like **The Elephant Man** or **The Straight Story**, he's as brilliant as any other.) In his chapter, Mike Leigh clearly explains the painstaking practice he goes through, working with actors for months to create truthful characters and situations before rolling the cameras – and even then the script is essentially written on set. Ken Loach, on the other hand, sticks closely to a script but conceals information about the story from his actors in order to elicit the most honest reactions from them. Lars von

Trier and Soderbergh have even lately taken to operating hand-held cameras themselves in an effort to be the very eye of the film and capture the drama in front of them first-hand. And when these master storytellers do capture truth in their work, the result is magical and affecting, whether it be **Breaking the Waves** or **The Piano, All About My Mother** or **Hana-bi, Ladybird Ladybird** or **Last Tango in Paris, Platoon** or **Eat Drink Man Woman, Secrets & Lies** or **Repulsion**. Having mastered the language and technicalities of the medium, these 15 directors are as close to artists as film-makers can be – striving to express themselves and achieve truth and beauty on their multi-dimensional canvas. That in many cases their films don't work shows how rare it is to achieve.

Of course, unlike painting, film is necessarily a collaborative medium. In the previous books in the series, film technicians discussed their craft and their relationships with film-makers. The directors in this book are no less deferential; Wim Wenders, Bernardo Bertolucci and Oliver Stone talk of their long collaborations with their respective cinematographers Robby Müller, Vittorio Storaro and Robert Richardson, although coincidentally in all three cases they have recently parted ways; James Ivory talks of his symbiotic 40-year partnership with Merchant and writer Ruth Prawer Jhabvala;

Ang Lee of his partnership with his producers Ted Hope and James Schamus, who is also his long-time screenwriter; Pedro Almodóvar and Takeshi Kitano of their respective composers Alberto Iglesias and Joe Hisaishi. All talk respectfully of the role of actors, although each has a different idea about their significance in the realisation of the film, ranging from reverence to slight disdain.

All the directors talked at length of the film-makers who came before them, inspired them or paved the way for them: Polanski cites British cinema of the '40s (Olivier, Powell and Pressburger); Wenders talks of Anthony Mann and John Ford; Bertolucci with vigour of the French *nouvelle vague* movement of the late '50s and '60s; Ivory with enormous respect of Satyajit Ray, with whom he collaborated on some of his early films in India. There is even appreciation crossover between the chapters. Soderbergh calls Lynch the only original in new US cinema, and Jane Campion also talks of Lynch and Wenders as early idols. Certainly the bedrock of intelligent contemporary cinema is European film in the '60s, whether it be France's *nouvelle vague*, the exciting Italian cinema of Fellini, Bolognini, Pasolini and Antonioni, the British 'kitchen sink' movement or the dazzling wave of film-makers from Soviet countries, such as Andrei Tarkovsky, Andrzej Wajda, Forman, Polanski and Kieslowski.

I was in conversation recently with the brilliant Nanni Moretti, who said that the film-makers of the '60s were ardent about getting their ideas, political and cinematic, onto film, whereas too many newcomers today are technically accomplished but "have nothing to say". Certainly the Hollywood system now tends to seek out commercial and music-video directors with a keen visual sense and leaves the risk-taking to the relatively new US independent movement kickstarted by Soderbergh's **sex, lies, and videotape** in 1989. Owned by profit-hungry multinationals, Hollywood's studios are now mainly focused on film tailored to the largest possible audience and refined by market researchers, a shame given that only 25 years ago, they were throwing their money behind Francis Ford Coppola, Hal Ashby, Martin Scorsese, William Friedkin, Robert Altman et al. That new market-driven film-making has, I believe, led Hollywood to underestimate the intelligence of audiences, whether in Middle America, Japan or Germany. Time and time again it is deemed a surprise when wide audiences respond to the distinctive voice of a film-maker. During the interview phase of the book, I met with Ang Lee while he was at the Cannes Film Festival 2000, having just completed **Crouching Tiger, Hidden Dragon**. Nobody could guess then that a year later the film would have grossed over $200 million at the worldwide box-office. Similarly, when I sat down with Steven

Soderbergh for the first time in L.A., I had just seen an early screening of **Traffic** – a project pooh-poohed by many in Hollywood as highbrow and "specialised". Two months later, it had become one of the biggest hits of the year. That both these films – bold, artistic visions, made with such confidence and control of the medium – scored huge commercial success, underlined for me the validity of exploring the craft of these two "stars" as well as 13 experts like them.

Fortunately for us, new directors with original voices from around the world are still supported by the non-Hollywood system, then discovered at auteur-centric film festivals like Cannes, Berlin, Venice, Toronto or Sundance. Hopefully this ever-renewed generation of film-makers can glean some inspiration from the insights on offer in this book, just like the subjects had their inspirations before them.

Such is the world of publishing that new films by the directors in the book will have been finished by the time 'Directing' is published. New work by Ken Loach (**The Navigators**), Steven Soderbergh (**Ocean's 11**), Pedro Almodóvar (**Talk to Her**), Roman Polanski (**The Pianist**) and possibly Mike Leigh (**Untitled 2001**) will have been screened to audiences. Sadly, the book had to stop somewhere.

I have received immeasurable help throughout the long process of putting the book together, in particular from my supportive editors at RotoVision, Erica Ffrench and Natalia Price-Cabrera, who eased me through some exasperating patches. Thank you also to the wonderful designers at Artmedia – Andrea Bettella and Francesca Wisniewska – to the patient transcriber Judith Burns at The Home Office and all at The Ronald Grant Archive for the kind use of their pictures. And a big thank-you to the people associated with the subjects who helped schedule interviews and source illustrations. They were Beth Binnard at Good Machine International, Isabelle Dassonville, Viccy Harper at Hilary Linstead & Associates, Caitlin Maloney, Ismail Merchant and Marla Shelton at Merchant Ivory Productions, Jacob Neiiendam, Rebecca O'Brien, Leigh Pickford and Sally Grant at Parallax Pictures, Paul Pflug at Artisan Entertainment, Gaye Pope and Jay Aaseng at Asymmetrical, Deborah Reade at Thin Man Films, Michel Ruben at El Deseo, Nancy Seltzer & Associates, Pia Severin at Zentropa, Jeremy Thomas and Alexandra Stone at Recorded Picture Co., Marla Ulrich at Wim Wenders Productions, Naoyuki Usui at Office Kitano and Rob Wilson at Ixtlan. Finally thank-you to my colleagues at *Screen International* and to my exceptional parents who have encouraged me in my love of film from a very early age.

MIKE GOODRIDGE

Pedro Almodóvar has become Spain's pre-eminent film-maker and one of the world's most distinctive and popular directors in his 13-film career, which began in 1980 with **Pepi, Luci, Bom... (Pepi, Luci, Bom y Otras Chicas del Montón)**. His trademark blend of high-passion melodrama, bawdy comedy, bold colour schemes and strong female characters developed throughout the '80s with, among others, **What**

pedro almodóvar

Have I Done to Deserve This? (Qué he hecho Yo Para Merecer Esto?, 1984), **Matador** (1985) and **Law of Desire (La Ley del Deseo**, 1987), reaching its zenith with **Women on the Verge of a Nervous Breakdown (Mujeres al Borde de un Ataque de Nervios**, 1988), which brought him international acclaim and an Oscar nomination. Throughout his work, Almodóvar has built a famous troupe of actors with whom he made multiple pictures, including Carmen Maura, Rossy de Palma, Antonio Banderas, Victoria Abril, Julieta Serrano, Chus Lampreave and others. The late '80s and '90s saw him make the less successful **Kika** (1993) and the controversial **Tie Me Up! Tie Me Down! (Atame!**, 1989), but also hits such as **High Heels (Tacones Lejanos**, 1991), **The Flower of My Secret (La Flor de Mi Secreto**, 1995) and **Live Flesh (Carne Trémula**, 1997). Perhaps his most perfect work was **All About My Mother (Todo Sobre Mi Madre**, 1999), which saw him finally make the move in critical and public perception from *enfant terrible* to established auteur. At time of going to press, he was in production on his 14th film. **Talk to Her (Hable con Ella)**.

interview

I had always been attracted to the idea of being involved in cinema since I was a very small child. I used to collect these photocards of film stars which I pasted in an album, and I really thought that the actors made the films and were responsible for what we saw on screen. So at that time, I really dreamed of being an actor. And really it wasn't until I was a teenager that I started to notice that there were other credits like screenwriter or director. Then I started to realise that there was someone behind the camera and that there was a voice behind the words of the actors telling them what to do. That's when I decided that that's what I really wanted to do. I wanted to be a storyteller, and cinema was the medium that I wanted to use to tell my stories. Actually my first vocation was to be a writer, and to this day I still have a great frustration at not having written a great novel.

I suppose all the movies that I've made are the novels that I've written. When I write, I try to involve the technicians and the actors in the story, and that is important because of my necessity of being understood. Actors have to have that

(1–9) **All About My Mother**: "When I was writing this film," remembers Almodóvar, "I cried a lot. It was this incredibly painful situation of a woman having a child and being present in his cycle of life and then watching him die in front of her eyes. The worst tragedy. For the death scene itself, I tried not to show everything but at the same time, I wanted to do something very strong. Originally I was going to make it an action sequence with stuntmen and specialists etc., but at the last minute I changed it because it was going to be too conventional and the conventional always makes me feel frustrated." (2, 5–6) Almodóvar on the set of **All About My Mother**.

7

8

9

All About My Mother: "Right after the accident, I could have gone to a scene with the mother crying, saying how it was his birthday but no, I cut to an empty hallway (7–9), the camera glides through the hallway and we get to the mother mute, her face swollen from crying. In fact, she doesn't even let the doctors talk. When they arrive and sit down in front of her, all they get to say is 'unfortunately...' and then we have this scream of pain. So I always go to the most essential, the most simple, which is sometimes the most difficult and transparent but the most effective."

information. They have the bonus of their bodies and their expression, but I am the watcher, the guardian of that. It's a game where there are laws which both of us respect. They have a certain freedom of action, but it's within a space of which I have marked the frontiers. To be honest, I don't think the actors I work with feel very free but I don't think they miss that freedom. For that, they have to have absolute confidence that my eyes are the best mirrors that they will have – and the only ones – and that those eyes will never betray them, they will be their best friend. I believe those actors come into that game with a lot of joy. I give them what they need so they don't need to do anything at home. In fact, I almost forbid them to learn their dialogue by heart. Of course, it's a great advantage for me that I've also written the script, because I can improve all the time and improvise during the rehearsals. The first time, I write it with a lot of drafts and I need it to really fit in perfectly and to be ironclad. I may improvise some of the reactions, some of the dialogue while shooting, but you can't improvise the structure.

So I fight with the screenplay for many months and when I'm finished and sure that everything is solid and I passionately want to do it – and sometimes, if I'm not passionate enough, I will discard it – we start thinking about the cast. With the cast you never know, because as we don't have many actors in Spain, I often have to adapt the script to the person we've cast. Agrado [in **All About My Mother**], for example, was at the beginning a real character who I remember when I was an adolescent living in Paris, and I had first discovered transvestites. Agrado was one of the oldest of these guys, who was over 40 and like an aunt to all of them. He helped the others make their dresses and put on their make-up and gave them great moral support. So the Agrado that I wanted to

portray in the film was a character of 45, an Agrado who has seen it all. But I couldn't find an actress or actor, and then when I met Antonia San Juan, we did a lot of rehearsals and she didn't have the tone I wanted, but I decided to leave her own tone and make the character younger. It's very simple – if there's something the actors do well, I'll try to make them do it. Victoria Abril cries very well, so I would try to make her character cry as much as possible in the movie.

We rehearse for about two weeks and the rehearsals help me to visualise the movie. Sometimes, the rehearsals are less for the actors than for me. It doesn't matter if the actors are very bad, I let them free; I don't work with them in character so much but more on the movement and, listening to them, I can realise when they are going to have difficulty with some specific dialogue or a specific scene, and I know I have to go and work on that scene.

When I'm shooting, the audience doesn't exist for me. I don't have room in my mind to think about other things. I feel like a medium at the service of the story and I do what the story demands. It sounds paranoid because the story is an abstract thing, but it becomes something very concrete for me and there is a very audible inner voice telling me what to do. I never get 100 per cent of what the story asks me, but I behave very obsessed just to get as much as possible. Even with someone as perfectionist as Stanley Kubrick, I don't think it's possible to get 100 per cent of what you want because 100 per cent includes many unconscious things you can't say. Even if you are an obsessive perfectionist, you are working constantly with human beings, and obviously they are going to change things because they are alive.

"It was very easy with both Jean-Paul Gaultier, the costume designer on **Kika** (1–4) and Ryuichi Sakamoto, the composer on **High Heels**. Gaultier is a great artist and he understood exactly what I wanted. He did the costumes incredibly well. And also when I corrected something, he was very understanding. Because stylists and musicians can have big egos. Sometimes it's difficult for me because they are serving the movie and my opinion, so they are not free, but if they have a completely different idea of what should be done, we fight. In both cases, they didn't want to change things, but they received more information and changed and improvised."

(1) Working with Agustin Almodóvar, his brother and producer: "I feel completely free because of him. Being free is a good thing because you feel completely responsible for what you do. There is a lot of loneliness too in responsibility, but that of course is the best situation for me to be in and I don't know if I can work any other way. I don't know if I'll work in English. I will do some day, but I don't know when. The language is a problem because I would need someone very close to me to adapt and write the dialogue. It could be a good experience to make a film in another language and to try and make everything mine, but of course how could it be completely, because it's another culture and another language? The way I think things up is usually rooted in my own experience or observation. (2–4) When the TV newscaster in **High Heels** announces a murder and then tells the world that she is a killer, obviously it's not part of my experience, but it's part of my imagination, which is also part of your experience. I took the first part from reality and then added the second part from my imagination. I take things from every place I can that is connected to my life, but it doesn't necessarily have to belong to my experience."

Lately I've been shooting a lot of takes in order to get the intensity I require from actors. Spanish is a very rich language in tones. So you can say "son of a bitch", but depending on your tone, on the music, it can be very flattering or an insult. I give the actors chances to say it in several different ways, just to see how it sounds. Sometimes, if you do it in three or four different ways, you discover things, and I also give them the chance to surprise me.

I try to avoid sentimentalism in my work, although there are a lot of feelings. I think **All About My Mother** is the antithesis of being sentimental. One of the things I'm most proud of in the film is that there are enormous time-lapses, ellipses where in fact I've managed to avoid sentimental scenes. Also, the acting is very sober. Cecilia [Roth] sometimes doesn't do anything with her face because I demand that, and it is very effective. I explained to her that her character was beyond pain, she has passed through that. The pain she has is so great that she doesn't feel it. So in this expressionless face, you see the pain even though she's not doing anything. That sobriety was the key to the success of the movie. People don't know why they identify so much with the characters, and since the beginning, working with the actors, I was conscious of that. I would tell them I don't know how to tell the story because what I'm telling is so crazy it's like a screwball comedy. It's a screwball drama. The idea was to do something with the mechanics of the plot and characters who belong in a screwball comedy, but make it completely serious. At the time, I was worried because it was something new for me.

It's difficult for me to talk about the colours and the music and the lighting in my films because I really make those decisions out of intuition and instinct. Looking back, I can come up with a theory as to why I chose certain themes, but while I'm working, the theory doesn't exist. Even though all of my films have bright colours, there have been graver tones coming into the later ones. Because I think the stories that I tell have also become graver. That use of colour and aesthetics in my films, even the language, has become ingrained in Spanish culture to such an extent that people talk about Almodóvarian things and restaurants and colours. Therefore I am very saturated with the Pedro Almodóvar aesthetic of the '80s and am trying to escape from that. In the '90s I escaped in my own way, so now I don't use a palette of soft-pop colours. In the last two movies, I used more black and white, which I've never used before. I definitely use intense and dramatic colours, but at this point I am more interested in the semitones – colours in-between other colours – rather than the primary colours.

There are two parts to the music. There are the songs which I discover before or during the scriptwriting process, and the score. The songs are part of the script and I always secure the rights to them before shooting, because they are so articulate with the words and the characters that I can't invent them. Sometimes they are songs that nobody knows. In **Live Flesh**, when the protagonist is in jail and he discovers that the girl of his dreams is the reason he is in jail, we played a song I had discovered before. That song becomes the voice of the character and the song says, "I want you to suffer like I suffer/ And I will learn to pray until I get that/I want you to feel as useless as a glass of whisky in your hand". I was very lucky to find it when I was writing. When it comes to the original score, on the last three movies, I have worked with Alberto Iglesias, who is a very easy character. Whenever I say no to

1

4

2

5

3

6

(1–13) Almodóvar's distinctive use of bright colours mark out his film-making style. Colours, he believes, both provoke and contain emotions, and he is specific about why he uses them. (1–6) "Green was a colour I was very afraid of until I started putting a soft green in **Tie Me Up! Tie Me Down!** and I liked it. Now when I use different tones of green, each time it is a new situation to use a colour I haven't used before." (7–10) Similarly, in **Live Flesh** he uses green in costume and the set design. (11–13) On other occasions, colour is used not thematically, but more for dramatic effect. For example, in **The Flower of My Secret**, when a distraught Marisa Paredes leaves her apartment, having just discovered that her husband has left her, she is dressed in blue and enters the street just as a medical protest is taking place. "They are all dressed in white robes and she in blue, and so in this sea of white, this woman stands out from the rest. It is the opposite of what she is feeling... Usually what I do at the beginning of a movie is make a selection of a palette of colours and that's the range we're going to work with on the sets – for the floors, the walls, the furniture, the costumes. I do all the design by myself, which is awful because I don't have the time and it makes me feel hysterical. I mix a lot of different styles. I always try to provoke emotions but I am never banal. I'm afraid this is a mixture which exists only inside my head."

7

11

8

12

9

13

10

(1–20) The title design and posters for his films are crucially important for Almodóvar, who works closely with designers to come up with the poster, press materials and advertising. He is frustrated when foreign distributors change the campaign he provides them, especially the US distributors who have very fixed ideas of how posters should look and almost never use graphic design. On his posters he has worked with some top Spanish designers including Ceesepe (**Pepi, Luci, Bom...** and **Law of Desire**), Carlos Berlanga (**Matador**), Ivan Zulueta (**Dark Habits, Labyrinth of Passion**), Juan Gatti (**Women on the Verge of a Nervous Breakdown, High Heels, Tie Me Up! Tie Me Down!, Kika, The Flower of My Secret** and **Live Flesh**) and Oscar Mariné (**All About My Mother**). He is a great admirer of Saul Bass and spends a lot of time on opening credits, such as these distinctive credits from **Women on the Verge of a Nervous Breakdown**, designed by Juan Gatti.

him or don't like what he's done, rather than inflate his ego or make him angry, it actually enriches him and gives him more information as to what I want and what he comes up with. On **All About My Mother**, Alberto was so moved by the film that he immediately went off and made five different demos, and when we played it with the image, I said, "absolutely no". He had started composing with the emotion he felt at the end of the movie, and it was like a requiem. I certainly didn't want to announce at the beginning that someone was going to die and that it was going to be a very painful film. I wanted the opposite of something dramatic – something subtle. Something that was almost a caress to the viewer, because in itself the place I was showing was already tough. So I told him this the second time and he understood, and this is the way we work.

I like all of my films. All of them have parts I adore and all of them have parts that I hate, including **All About My Mother**. **Law of Desire** is the one that I feel most proud of, because at the time it was very difficult to do. I am very happy with **Women on the Verge of a Nervous Breakdown**, which is one of the ones which came out closest to how I wanted. All 13 that I've made have been important. I don't have that feeling that each one has taken me on another step. All of them take part in the same territory and all of them were very important to me at the moment of doing them.

I don't feel that I am totally content as a film-maker but I do think I am developing and learning what I want. That is the situation I am in now. I think I can only be myself in a more radical way. My focus is almost more narrow with age in the sense that I know more about what I want and the way I want to tell a story. Far from opening up my horizons, the more I

work, the more I get a sense that I can only make the stories that interest me in a very specific way, the things that move me in a very personal way. There are many possibilities in this small place where I am, but they have to do with the life that I am living now. They can offer me 100 scripts, and even if they are amazing I won't do them because I am only interested in specific things. There is only one option for me, and it is inside me.

biography

Born in 1933 in Paris, Roman Polanski has had one of the most extraordinary careers, and indeed lives, of all living film-makers. A survivor of the Nazi holocaust which killed his mother (he and his family moved to Poland just before the advent of the Second World War), he became a teenage celebrity in films such as Andrzej Wajda's first film, **A Generation (Pokolenie)**. In 1954, he went to Lodz Film

roman polanski

School, but moved back to Paris in 1960, then returning to Poland to make his first feature, the outstanding **Knife in the Water**. It introduced themes of isolation, paranoia, alienation and violence that would recur in Polanski's next few films – a series of disturbing masterpieces including **Repulsion** (1965), **Cul-de-Sac** (1966), **The Fearless Vampire Killers** (1967), his first film in Hollywood **Rosemary's Baby** (1968) and **Macbeth** (1971). His biggest triumph is probably **Chinatown** (1974), still considered one of the best American films of the '70s, if not of all time. He returned to Europe to direct **The Tenant** in 1976, in which he also excelled in the lead role, and a superlative adaptation of 'Tess of the D'Urbévilles', called **Tess** in 1980. His films since then, including **Frantic** (1988), **Bitter Moon** (1992), **Death and the Maiden** (1994) and **The Ninth Gate** (1999), have been disappointing, although always interesting. His next film, an adaptation of Wladyslaw Szpilman's 'The Pianist', sees him address the holocaust which overshadowed his own childhood for the first time.

interview

I consider putting a script together as the first stage of directing a movie. How can you build an edifice, how can you build a skyscraper without a blueprint? You have to know what your plan is, so to a certain extent not only in pre-production but during writing you have to know what are the limits of the medium at your disposal. Making a film is so technical – it's not painting or composing music. You have to decide at least what your format is going to be – whether it's going to be black and white or colour, what kind of technicians you plan to use, the length of it, the style. All this involves a lot of technical decisions even at script stage.

I'm not good with writing, I write because I have to, but I neither like nor excel at it. But I need to be involved in screenplay-writing because it disciplines my idea of the movie to come. I am convinced that a director should have the model of the movie in his head before he comes on the set. Shooting is just an execution of that plan. There are plenty of people who have fabulous imaginations, but few are capable of making it material so that others are able to partake in their

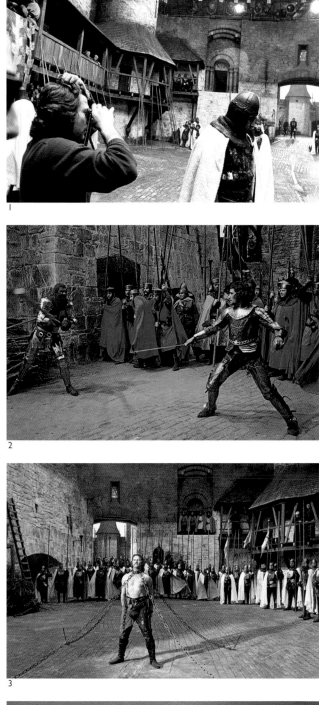

1

2

3

4

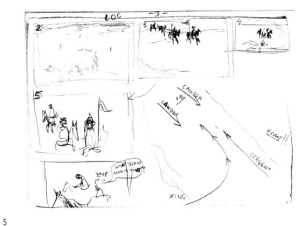

5

6

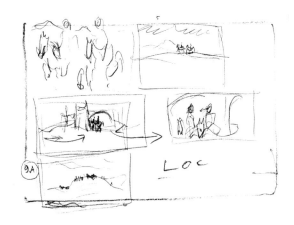

7

8

3. EXT. BATTLEFIELD. DAY

A royal party on horseback appears in the distance. The colours of
their robes and banners contrast with the sullen greyness of the
scene. This is KING DUNCAN, flanked by his sons MALCOLM and
DONALBAIN, and followed by LENNOX, ANGUS, TWO GROOMS and
ATTENDANTS with banners.

SOLDIERS kneel as the party passes.

4. EXT. BATTLEFIELD. DAY

Three horsemen approach from the opposite direction: a SERGEANT
with a terrible wound in the face, and two other SOLDIERS. They
stop and salute the KING as he passes.

5. EXT. BATTLEFIELD. DAY

                    KING
              (looking at the
               SERGEANT)
         What bloody man is that?

                  MALCOLM
              Hail, brave friend!

He beckons to the SERGEANT, who rides up to the KING.

                  MALCOLM
         Say to the King thy knowledge of the broil
         As thou didst leave it.

Wiping away the blood, the SERGEANT tries to make light of his
injuries and deliver a normal military report.

                  SERGEANT
         Doubtful it stood. The merciless
                              Macdonald
         Led his rebellion from the Western isles,
         And fortune on his damned quarrel smiled:
         But brave Macbeth --

                  SOLDIER
              (cutting in)
         -- Well he deserves that name! --

6. Contd.

The royal party rides up to them. All look at the captive.

                  ROSS
            God save the King!

                  KING
         What news, my worthy thane?

                  ROSS
              (indicating CAWDOR)
         Norway himself with terrible numbers,
         Assisted by this most disloyal
                              traitor,
         The Thane of Cawdor, began a dismal
                              conflict,
         Till that Bellona's bridegroom, bold
                              Macbeth,
         Confronts the King, rebellious arm 'gainst
                              arm,
         Curbing his lavish spirit - and, to conclude,
         The victory fell on us.

                  KING
            Great happiness!

He spurs his horse and rides on with his party, but soon wheels round
and shouts:

                  KING
         No more that Thane of Cawdor shall
                              deceive
         Our bosom interest! Go, pronounce
                              his present death,
         And with his former title greet Macbeth!

7. EXT. ROADSIDE. (GALLOWS). DUSK.

MACBETH, on horseback, motionless, staring intently. He is young,
with an open, honest face.

He is looking at a long scaffold, erected by the roadside. SOLDIERS
are ready to hang two dozen bound PRISONERS by hauling them up on
pulleys. OTHER TROOPS look on. BANQUO, also on horseback,
raises his sword. He brings it down in a signal of command and the
hanging begins.

MACBETH, having seen enough, wheels his horse and rides off up the
gentle slope of a hill overlooking the road.

7. Contd.

BANQUO surveys the executions, turns and, seeing that MACBETH
has ridden off, follows him.

8. EXT. HILLSIDE TO RUIN. DUSK

MACBETH trotting along the brow of the hill. BANQUO joins him, and
they ride in silence. Rain starts to fall.

9. EXT. RUIN. DUSK

Rain is falling heavily. MACBETH and BANQUO ride up to a ruined
abbey with an archway that offers shelter. They halt under the arch
and sit in silence looking ahead.

9a. EXT. DISTANT VALLEY. DUSK

Far below in the valley a column of FOOTSOLDIERS winds, followed
by carts loaded with provisions.

9b. EXT. RUIN. DUSK

                  MACBETH
         So foul and fair a day I have not seen.

Suddenly both their horses shy. The two men exchange puzzled looks.
A strange toneless crooning comes from further back in the ruins.
BANQUO moves his horse to investigate. He sees a woman, squatting
with her back to him, milking a goat.

As he approaches she turns towards him but does not speak. Her mouth
gapes toothlessly, her hair is matted, and she wears filthy rags:
clearly she is ancient. This is the FIRST WITCH.

BANQUO, curious, moves a little closer, and notices two more women
around a corner. One of them, as aged as the first, is kneeling and
massaging a dark ointment into the shoulders of an ugly, pudgy, vacant-
looking girl, who is sorting through herbs in a basket on her lap. She
is crooning. Both have their backs to BANQUO. As he approaches their
heads turn towards him. The elder of the pair is the BLIND WITCH;
the girl is the YOUNG WITCH.

BANQUO's horse rears up. The YOUNG WITCH titters.

                  BANQUO
              (to MACBETH)
         What are these,
         So withered and so wild in their attire,
         That look not like the inhabitants of the earth
         And yet are on it?

12

13

14

(1–14) **Macbeth**: Polanski wanted to make a movie of a Shakespeare play since he had seen Laurence Olivier's **Hamlet**. He shot his version of 'Macbeth' on location in Scotland, complete with a murder sequence which is still shocking today. "The film was a serious adaptation – even if it was co-financed by *Playboy* – and I had a fabulous collaborator in Ken Tynan, who wrote the script with me. He was such a scholar of Shakespeare, was so secure with the material, that we reviewed every single word that was uttered, and every scene was inspired by what we supposed the author wanted to say. Shakespeare is a little like jazz in that you can do with it what you feel fit because there are no directions. It was very badly received in America, as I think the critics felt safer about putting it down as they were not secure reviewing Shakespeare. In England, however, it was extremely well-received. They know more about it, after all." (5–11) Polanski's storyboard and shooting script for the opening scenes of the film.

CORSO is impressed but does his best not to show it.

                    CORSO
          May I take a look?

                    BALKAN
          That's why I brought you here.

He goes over to the 'monolith' and punches a keyboard on a control panel. The sheet of tinted plate glass glides aside with a faint hum.

CORSO, who has joined him, adjusts his glasses for a closer look. His eyes roam along the spines of the books.

                    BALKAN (cont.)
          Beautiful, aren't they? That soft
          sheen, that superb gilding... Not
          to mention the centuries of wisdom
          they contain... I know people who
          would kill for a collection like
          this. (CORSO shoots him a quick
          glance) The Ars Diavoli! You'll
          never see as many books on the
          subject anywhere else in the world.
          They're the rarest, the choicest
          editions in existence. It has taken
          me a lifetime to assemble them.
          Only the supreme masterpiece was
          missing. Come...

Gesturing to CORSO to follow him, he goes over to an ultra-modern, brushed steel lectern standing beside one of the huge picture windows.

As he approaches the lectern, CORSO briefly glimpses the sheer drop beyond the plate glass, the twinkling lights of traffic passing in the street far below.

Reposing on the lectern is a black book adorned with a gold pentacle. CORSO opens it at the title page, which displays the title in Latin and an emblem consisting of A TREE ENCIRCLED BY A SERPENT DEVOURING ITS OWN TAIL.

                    CORSO
          (not looking at BALKAN)
          'The Nine Gates of the Kingdom of
          Shadows...'

                    BALKAN
          You're familiar with it?

                    CORSO
          Sure. Venice, 1666. The author and
          printer was Aristide Torchia, burned
          by the Holy Inquisition, together
          with all his works. Only three copies
          survived.

                    BALKAN
          One.

                    CORSO
          The catalogs list three copies surviving
          in private ownership: the Fargas, the
          Kessler, and the Telfer.

                    BALKAN
          True. You know your business, but you're
          mistaken nonetheless. According to my
          own research, only one is authentic.

                    CORSO
          Well, three are known.

                    BALKAN
          That's the trouble.

CORSO resumes his inspection of the book.

                    CORSO
          Where did you get it?

                    BALKAN
          I bought it from Telfer.

                    CORSO
          (surprised)
          Telfer?

                    BALKAN
          (looking out of the window)
          Yes, he finally sold it to me. The day
          before he killed himself.

                    CORSO
          Good timing.

BALKAN ignores this. CORSO carefully turns the pages. He lingers over AN ENGRAVING OF A KNIGHT IN ARMOR RIDING TOWARD A CASTLE WITH A FINGER TO HIS LIPS. Below it a caption. BALKAN draws closer and reads it aloud over CORSO's shoulder:

                    BALKAN
          'Silentium est aureum.'

(1–7) **The Ninth Gate** is a loose adaptation of a novel called 'The Club Dumas' by Arturo Pérez-Reverte. "It has two plots with several subplots and a lot of digressions, and it's told by several narrators. Making a movie out of it required some drastic cuts and decisions, because it's not a novel that can be filmed as is. A motion picture requires much more discipline and rigourous construction." The novel involves two stories – one about the search for a lost chapter of 'The Three Musketeers', the other the lost manuscript of 'The Nine Gates to the Kingdom of Shadows' – which interweave throughout the book. Polanski and his co-writers focused only on the latter. (4, 6) Extracts from the script of **The Ninth Gate** and (5, 7), two of the woodcuts from the book within the film.

fantasy. A director's talent is to be able to share his imagination with the audience.

I do a lot of preparation. I don't storyboard, because that cramps my style. I used to storyboard my short films because it was a natural way for me to come up with a usable script. I went to an art school and had more talent for drawing than writing. But when I started my first feature [**Knife in the Water**], I realised that the storyboard was making me go in the wrong direction. When you come on set you confront the reality, which is not necessarily the way you have storyboarded or imagined it. You discover life richer than your imagination. I only storyboard when I have to share certain ideas with a great number of people for a big complex scene or a shot with special effects. When you have special effects, you can't improvise. You have to discuss it to the utmost detail with technicians and they have to know what the camera angle is going to be etc. But when you have something like a love scene or a fight, it's better to let the actors rehearse on the set and see what they come up with, and then film it.

I am spontaneous on set, but what is important to me is to be as close to my pre-imagined model as possible. The encounter with reality makes it difficult, because reality modifies your original concept and superimposes itself on it in such a way that finally you have practically forgotten your blueprint. I make a constant effort to remember how I have imagined a particular scene, how I saw it. Maybe the actors aren't like the characters I've imagined. Even if you write with a particular actor in mind, that person is always a little different on the set. I know when I'm improving on my original idea or screwing it up. The more contained the film is, like **Death and the Maiden**, the easier it is to stick to your model. **The**

Ninth Gate was quite far from my original concept for several reasons. First, I did not imagine the central character to be the way Johnny [Depp] interpreted it. I wanted him to be a little bit more exuberant. In the film you have that central character going through a series of events surrounded by very colourful secondary characters, and I imagined him as exuberant as everyone else. But Johnny played it sort of flat and straightforward and, to some degree, humourless. It made me wonder for the first couple of days, but after that I decided to let him develop it his way. In my model, the humour was more obvious than it comes across in the movie. I think ultimately the humour is too subtle.

In my films, I adhere more or less to the Greek concept of a play. I can't talk about it in very eloquent terms because I always did these things instinctively; I only later realised that I was simply doing things that have been done by people for thousands of years. Although I hate this religious division into three acts so dear to Hollywood executives, who call themselves creative, I must admit there is something to it.

In **The Ninth Gate**, the set-up is in New York. That is the first act, and the second act is everything that happens until the hero finds the society of devil worshippers. And then there is the culmination in the castle. Of course one of the greatest difficulties in making a movie is that it's made up of little pieces and when the director gets too distracted by a particular scene or shot, he loses contact with the rest. I think the main two problems film-makers face are a) to figure out how the piece of the puzzle will fit the rest, and b) where to put the camera. When you're watching a movie and you feel uncomfortable and everything seems awkward, it's because the director didn't know where to put the camera and just filmed it from a wrong angle. And if you don't get satisfaction from the whole movie, it's because the pieces don't fit together. On stage, a play can be excruciating, but it involves you because there is always clear continuity. It's been run through many, many times before it was presented to you. In a movie, you rehearse it a few times and then shoot it completely out of sequence.

Writing a script, it's important to have clearly in mind the point of view from which the story is told. If it's shown from one character's point of view, it's always more effective than being all over the place. It's the same with filming. In **Bitter Moon**, for example, there is a scene where Peter Coyote is being hit by a car. He is in a taxi with two girls, one decides to leave and in an effort to run after her, he gets out of the car on the street side and is hit by an oncoming van. The stuntman prepared the scene and had a lot of ideas how to film it and good angles where one could really see the impact. So did the director of photography. But I was all the while convinced that it should be seen from the interior of the taxi. The camera should be with Coyote, and so when he opens the door and steps out, boom, the van hits him. Nevertheless we put a couple of cameras outside and did it from a number of angles. When I saw the rushes, it was clear that my angle was the right one. You really felt how the guy would feel. It's a different experience watching it from the road or the pavement. If the van comes at him and you see him fly over the bonnet, it's not so unexpected.

In a film like **Tess**, it's entirely different because you're not always with the central character. The story is more epic, and therefore you know you can show it from your point of view because you're narrating. In **Rosemary's Baby**, however,

Rosemary narrates. You don't quite know what's happening to her, but you're with her and you're going through the events with her. You mustn't cut to the other end of the telephone line and show the guy she's talking to. That's nothing new, of course. It had been done before by a great number of film-makers and writers. **Rosemary's Baby** had a certain ambiguity. That's what I liked about the novel, and I amplified that in the film. It could be read in various ways. The suspicions of Rosemary could be unfounded and simply a figment of her imagination. There's nothing supernatural about the story except the story itself. You may see the devil in what's supposed to be her dream, and her dreams relate to the witches' coven where she was carried for some kind of ritual. But even if the coven exists, the devil is never shown. She thinks she is dreaming and at one moment she says, "this is not a dream, this is really happening".

Rosemary's Baby and **Repulsion** worked, not because there was tension on the set – in fact we had a lot of laughs on set – but because I stuck to my blueprint. The atmosphere in those movies is the way I imagined it and as I was working on the set I tried to render it. I saw perfectly well where each scene fits with the rest. That fitting is the clue to it all. You can try to heighten the suspense in the editing room by playing with the rhythm of the narration.

On **Rosemary's Baby** and on **Chinatown**, I was protected by the head of the studio, Robert Evans. When he chose a director, he did it because he trusted the man and would give him the opportunity to show his abilities. It's not the way things are now. You have this creative group I mentioned who send you notes and who remind me of a bunch of precocious children. They're so arrogant. They make me think of students

(1–4) Famously, Polanski and his **Chinatown** screenwriter Robert Towne couldn't agree on the ending to the film. "I can't remember how it all happened, but we parted ways before shooting began and I started the picture without the ending or the love scene between Jack Nicholson and Faye Dunaway (3), because Bob didn't want them to sleep together, and I thought it was important for the film. I thought they should have an intimate moment and then the girl should die. When I was about three-quarters of the way through, Bob Evans [the producer] said that he had to have an ending. And first we had to insert this love scene, so I wrote that and we shot it. And at this point, I had a knife to my throat and I had to come up with an ending, so I asked Dick Sylbert [the production designer] to find a street that would look like Chinatown. As there was no Chinatown in L.A., we chose a street with a few Chinese restaurants, and Dick did the rest and I wrote the scene. So we prepared for it, and then I gave it to Jack Nicholson to rewrite his dialogue in his style before we went ahead and shot the scene. You see, Bob Towne had this fantastic ear for dialogue, and he made Jack's lines sound like Jack speaks in life." (4) Polanski himself had a famous role in the film as the hoodlum who slices into Nicholson's nose with a flick-knife. (1) Polanski with lead Jack Nicholson and (2) Faye Dunaway.

4

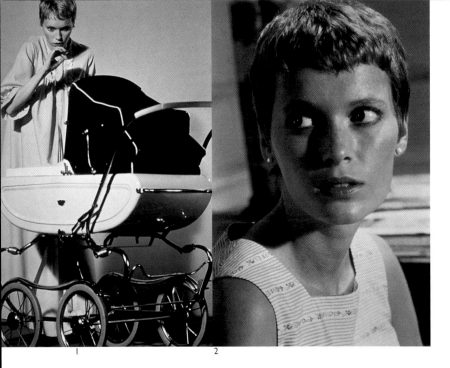

(1–6) Polanski's great horror movie, and one of the all-time classics of the genre, is **Rosemary's Baby**, although he prefers to refer to it as a "suspense film". Still terrifying to this day for what it doesn't show, the film was adapted by Polanski from Ira Levin's novel, and is considered the precursor for the satanic horror movies of the '70s such as **The Exorcist** and **The Omen**. (4–5) Polanski on the set of **Rosemary's Baby**.

6

who want to say something on a subject they know nothing about. Now I protect myself by producing my own films. But it's hard. The more time you spend on activities unrelated to directing, the more the film suffers. Many American journalists ask me about **Chinatown** because they consider it was my best picture made in America, but, aside from the fact that it was a great script, it was the only film I can remember where I was left completely alone with no worries, no scheduling problems, no budgeting. Robert Evans was the producer and head of studio and he gave me complete freedom of action. I had nothing to worry about. All my energy went into the right channels. As for working with actors, I have no method. Actors are people, and all people are different. Every actor requires a specific approach. There are some who need coaxing, others need tension and conflict. Some of them like you to show them what you want, others hate it and feel offended. There is absolutely no recipe.

I'm never nervous when I work. I remember when I was in the first or second year of Lodz Film School and made my first short film. I couldn't sleep the night before shooting. Then I was really nervous and it was a fabulous feeling. Unfortunately that's gone. I remember driving into Paramount Studios on my first day of **Rosemary's Baby** and I was completely relaxed. I had no butterflies in the stomach. I wish I could experience the same excitement I had when I was doing my first short. (Ironically, my first film was never finished. It was during the Communist period, and my rushes were developed with some Soviet documentary and sent to Moscow by mistake. I never got them back.)

I never think of the audience when I'm making a movie. I am my own audience. I make movies to satisfy the movie-goer in me. I go to the movies a lot, and I suspect that the choice of my subjects comes from what I would like to see in the theatre. I sort of cater to my own taste. Once I have an idea, I imagine it the way that would satisfy the spectator in me. As a movie-goer, I don't consider myself special. I'm under the illusion, a very naïve illusion sometimes, that everybody else will share my taste. If they don't like a film I've made, I feel tremendously surprised, and very often they don't. Sometimes they like it too late. **The Tenant**, for example, was a total flop when it came out but has now become a sort of cult film. The same with **Cul-de-Sac**.

To conclude, it's all really about storytelling. I think you have to know how to tell a story. It doesn't matter whether it's a movie or a joke over dinner. There are people who start telling a joke, and you cringe. Others open their mouths and you're hanging on their every word.

biography

To the rest of the world he may be a renowned actor and director of award-winning films, but in Japan, Takeshi Kitano, a.k.a Beat Takeshi, is a multimedia star and celebrity with his own weekly primetime TV show, columns in magazines and newspapers, a total of 55 published novels, books of essays and poetry to his credit, and a background in stand-up comedy which saw him perform in clubs and theatres for a

takeshi kitano

decade during the '70s and '80s. He started acting in films in 1981 and worked with, among others, Nagisa Oshima in **Merry Christmas, Mr Lawrence** (1983) and more recently **Gohatto** (2000). In 1989 he made his directorial debut with **Violent Cop (Sono Otoko Kyobo ni Tsuki)** and has been a prolific film-maker since then, delivering a string of violent portraits of cops and crooks such as **Boiling Point (3–4x Jugatsu,** 1990) and **Sonatine** (1993), interspersed with more tender character studies such as **Kids Return** (1996) and **A Scene at the Sea (Ano Natsu, Ichiban Shizukana Umi,** 1991). His greatest triumph to date was **Hana-bi** (1997), or **Fireworks** as it was called in English, a melancholy blend of shocking violence and poignant disaffection, themes which infect all Kitano's work. **Hana-bi** sealed his worldwide reputation, snaring the Golden Lion at the Venice Film Festival in 1997. Since then he has made the heartbreaking **Kikujiro** (1999) and **Brother** (2000), his first English-language film which was set among organised-crime gangs in L.A. Since **Violent Cop**, Kitano has written all his films, edited most of them and played the lead role in five.

interview

I never wanted to be a film-maker when I was younger. It just so happened that **Violent Cop** was supposed to be directed by another director, Kinji Fukasaku, but he felt he had to drop out because of my inconsistent availability and my inability to stick with the schedule that he demanded of me, so someone came up with the idea that I direct it myself, and I thought why not. It was a happy accident. It was somebody else's original and the script was already written, so once it was decided that I was going to direct the film, I changed it considerably to my taste, imagining what I would like to see if I were the audience of the film.

The way I conceive a film is to come up with the four stages or images of the film like a four-strip cartoon in a comic. Introduction, development of the story, twists and turns of the plot and punchline. It's a very rough idea of just four images. I don't go lock myself away for a month when I'm writing. Sometimes I come up with a scene when I'm out drinking with a friend or on the golf course, and I just take a note of it in a notebook. In any case, the four images act as the backbone of

1

2

3

4

5

(1–5) **Hana-bi**: (1–2) Kitano used his own oil paintings in **Hana-bi** doubling as the work of Horibe, the paralysed cop played by Ren Osugi. "When I had a motorbike accident, I was devastated by the effects of it and I had nothing to do because I couldn't return to the TV show again until I fully recovered, so I started painting as a hobby. So that character contains quite a few autobiographical elements." (4–5) Kitano directs himself in the opening fight scene from **Hana-bi** (discussed on page 43).

the story, and a lot of the detail comes when I'm shooting. After the four images, I divide the shots or order the sequences in my mind and play it like a film on a projector in my head. I see the film in my head, and after that the shooting and editing are just the way of realising those ideas.

Sometimes I make mistakes and what I had in mind doesn't come across in the actual film. That's often in the performances of the actors – and that includes me – and I get disappointed at watching the footage that I have shot because it seems so different to what I had in mind. There are other things like special effects which often don't have the quality that I had visualised before. But making a film is like making porcelain to me. The rush of the film is in the way it changes depending on the lighting or the weather, just like porcelain, that can be changed into a totally different shape depending on the temperature of the fire or the material. A film is a very sensitive thing. Some things turn out how I imagined them, and some things, even though the temperature was right and the lighting was perfect on set, disappoint my expectations. It's ambiguous.

I usually stick to the first take. It's like going to the zoo and seeing unusual animals like a panda bear or a koala bear. If you see them every day, you get bored watching them but the first impression has a major impact. That's why I stick to one take, two at most. I sometimes tell the actors that we're rehearsing and then ask the cinematographer to roll the cameras and use that as a take and move on to the next shot. When I do this, because it would be too impolite to move on straight away to the next shot, I roll it again for the sake of the actors. So in the end I have two takes of the same shot, but I mostly choose the first one from the supposed rehearsal shot.

When I'm directing a film, even though I am originally an actor, what's most important to me is what will be on the film, so I don't really care about how the actors want to come up with their characters and their backgrounds. That stuff doesn't mean anything to me if the actor does a horrible job in the film. It's possible to make films with animal characters. You don't instruct cats and dogs on what their motivation is or how to behave in a situation. If I can make animal films without verbal collaboration between actors and directors, I don't mind shooting actors in the frame and moving on, without worrying about what kind of mood they are in. In that respect, the actors in my films have a lot of freedom to do what they like, and if I don't like what they do, I'll change the angle of the camera rather than correct them with detailed instructions. In other words, rather than get the actors to move as I wish, I tend to move myself as a director somewhere.

When I work as an actor on films for other directors now, I respect them a lot more. What I've learned is that one of the things a director hates most is when the actor says his or her character should move or be like this and try and have a say on the direction of the actors. So since I started directing films myself, my policy is to do what the director tells me when I'm acting for him. As for directing myself, I use stand-in actors during the rehearsal of the shot so that I can work out how the camera should move, and then analyse what I don't like about the stand-in's performance and movements and the way he says the dialogue. Then when I'm in front of the camera I try to correct those things and try not to be bad. What often happens is that I am behind the camera during the rehearsal and using my stand-in, and after the rehearsal is over, I'll start to move on to the next shot. I am so absorbed that I forget we have to shoot it with me in front of the camera!

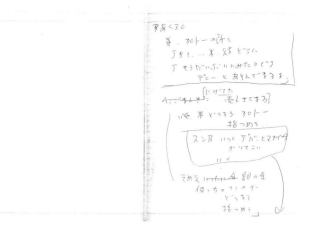

(1–12) Kitano's 2000 gangster movie **Brother** was largely set in L.A., and its dialogue was mainly English, a first for Kitano who not only acted in English but directed English-speaking actors using a translator. (3–4) Kitano, who speaks little English, says he focused on the actors' facial expressions and movements and let bilingual crew-members listen carefully to the dialogue and report back to him on whether they were "OK". As for his vision of America, he treated the American characters as "symbolic images" of what his characters imagined them to be. "I could have made extensive research on modern-day America and be as true as possible to the real America, but that would lead to the same mistakes I see in American movies, where the way Japanese people are depicted is so untrue. Conversely, I shot the Japanese sequences in as realistic a way as possible to contrast the detailed way the lead character sees Japan with America, which to him is like some illusion." (5–6, 9–10) Kitano avoided shooting familiar tourist sites in his vision of L.A. "It was my conscious choice to avoid any postcard locations. There was a basic tone I wanted in terms of look. Every location I chose was some sort of nowhere-ville – somewhere which reminds people of nowhere, and I wanted that tone." (1–2, 7–8, 11–12) Kitano's initial ideas for a shooting script.

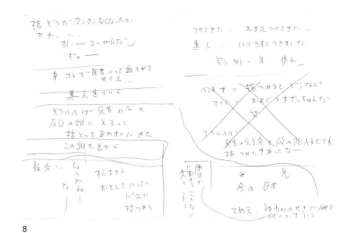

7

8

9

10

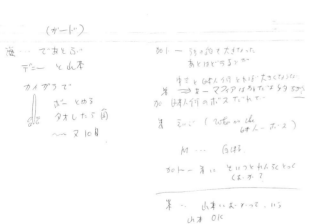

11

12

Unusually, I shoot in sequence, and this can be difficult for the art department or prop people. During the shooting of **Hana-bi**, for example, Ren Osugi who plays Nishi's colleague, improvised and said, "why don't I buy a beret at this point?", so I cut and addressed everyone and said in the first scene tomorrow, we need a beret.

Once the shooting has started, I let the film follow my ideas as we go in sequence, and I like the film to get its direction itself. It tends to be me who is playing the leading character, so this character I play leads the way that the film goes emotionally. I'd like to make a very happy, optimistic film one day but so far they just can't be like that. The films are all sad because my view of life in general is like that. Objectively I've achieved a lot in my career; I'm a household TV personality in Japan and a cultural figure and I have a standing in the international film field which I feel honoured by, but ultimately these accolades are nothing to me. I can't be optimistic because my thoughts are not, and that is reflected in the films.

Many of the characters are pressured by the environment they are currently in and have to go on a trip to get out of that. That's what motivates the characters in my films to go on journeys. Kikujiro probably uses the boy as the reason for his own search for his mother, and to experience the things that he could not experience when he was a child. Likewise the boy needs Kikujiro's help in order to find his mother. What's interesting to me is that they have the same aim but what they find after the journey is exactly the same kind of sadness.

On a similar line, in many of the characters I play, two opposite elements become one. I often use the theory that a character is like a pendulum swinging on both sides – from violence on one side to affection and emotion on the other. It's like the potential energy theory in physics. If you have 100 per cent power of violence in you, you can swing it to the 100 per cent power to do violent things. But if you only have ten per cent power of violence, you can easily swing over to 90 per cent on the other side. I want to depict violence and tenderness as one and the same, like a swinging pendulum.

Not all my films involve violence, and obviously whether or not there is violent content depends on the concept and the script, but in the end I suppose all the films in one way or another deal with life and death. It's inescapable that I deal with this. Up until **Hana-bi**, most of the scenes with fighting and gunplay were based on real stories I had been told when I was a child, because I grew up in a very working-class section of Tokyo, and there were a lot of Yakuza-type men and street punks hanging around. I've witnessed violence like that with my own eyes and heard the stories myself, and **Hana-bi** is based on one of them.

The way I depict the violence itself is similar to what I do in my comic routines. Often what makes comedy funny is to give the audience something very familiar to them, something very ordinary, and then all of a sudden put something unexpected in there. That's what makes people laugh. So if you apply that to the violent scenes in my films, you know it happens in the most unlikely situations. That gives it a stronger impact than a setting where you would expect there to be a lot of violence. Ever since I've been doing stand-up comedy, I've always mocked the clichés of film. It's like in a suspense thriller when the perpetrator of the crime always confesses to the beautiful leading lady that he was the killer just before the

(1) Kitano has worked consistently with composer Joe Hisaishi, whose haunting and evocative scores have perfectly complemented Kitano's melancholy drama. "Up until **Hana-bi**, I let him come up with the music he wanted and it worked like boxing sparring. I would come up with some rushes and challenge him to come up with some music to go with it. But on **Kikujiro**, I had a specific preference for the music. I wanted the music to be like George Winston's 'Summer', so I had a meeting with Mr Hisaishi and told him that was what I wanted. That's the only film where I have given the composer specific instruction (2–3)."

(1–4) "I use the beach scene in all my films and I keep going back to the beach metaphor, because human beings are the most evolved life form, and all the living creatures came from the sea. In ancient times, there was a very simple bacteria which went on to evolve into fish and then moved onto land and evolved into the human being. And if the human being is the most advanced in evolution of all living creatures, by putting him on the beach, it gives you a strange tension between the ocean and the human. With all the material complications that the characters face, it's as if the ocean is questioning the human and asking, 'Are you really that evolved after all these years?' I like that tension. I never let the characters swim joyously. I just make them stand in front of it." Stills from (1) **Kikujiro**, (3) **A Scene at the Sea** and (4) **Brother**. (2) Kitano directing on a beach for **A Scene at the Sea**.

good guy catches up with him. I always make fun of these scenes in my stand-up routine, and that is specifically what I try to avoid when I'm making a film.

I feel that I avoided those clichés successfully in the opening scene of **Hana-bi**, where the main character encounters two punk-like juvenile delinquents and fights with them. The way I structured the editorial sequence of that shot was satisfying to me. I think I will construct my films in the future more or less like the opening scene of **Hana-bi**, which I like, as it omitted certain elements. It's been a hundred years since cinematography was invented, and it's about time we put a little faith or trust in the viewer's expectations. So in that scene, I had two guys who obviously showed hostility to each other. Should I show them fighting? No. What I did was to show them standing confronting each other and the next shot is one of them on the floor. Viewers can imagine that there has been a fight between the two shots. If I had physically shown them fighting, it would look like a kung-fu movie which has been done so many times before by other people. I'd rather let the audience imagine what happens. It's like one of those TV programmes in Japan about food where people savour the food and think it's delicious. But once the commentator explains exactly how the soup was made or what ingredients cause that flavour, they lose interest. The more you unnecessarily explain things, the more people lose interest.

In terms of the technicalities of film-making, I'm still not convinced that I am a professionally equipped film director. For the last few years, my films have been quite popular in Europe and other parts of the world, and since I've started going to film festivals and being interviewed by journalists, I've felt that I should be able to answer some of these technical questions. That's why I started to watch the old movies of Kurosawa and others, because until then I hadn't seen any of the great movies. However, I do get the feeling that once I start thinking in terms of cinema technique, I might start copying other directors and repeat what others have done before me. So in some respects I'm not too crazy about acquiring cinema technique or grammar. I make the films I want to make with complete artistic freedom. I don't think much of their box-office potential because I consider my many endeavours like a double insurance policy. When I make films, I convince myself that my real profession after all is as a comedian, so it's not like I have to compromise artistically to make money out of them. I can make a living doing all these TV shows so I don't need to change the films to suit the needs of the audience. Then again, when I'm doing the TV show I find myself thinking in the same way. I can make my own films and I can make a living out of that side, so I don't have to worry about the popularity of the TV show. It's like a double insurance policy on both sides.

Actually I have a third insurance policy recently, and that is my wife, who has saved all the money I earned through the TV shows and films I've appeared in over the last 20 years, and she's got a huge savings account. Maybe I don't have to do anything after all. She's got enough savings for me. But then again, what if she dumps me and takes all the money?

Mike Leigh occupies a unique position on the world stage. His extraordinarily rigourous process of film-making by rehearsal, instinct and improvisation involves extensive commitments from actors and crew members but has resulted in some of the most truthful and insightful character studies of the last two decades. Trained as an actor at the Royal Academy of Dramatic Arts (RADA) and then at the London

mike leigh

interview

Film School, Leigh made his feature-directing debut in 1971 with **Bleak Moments**, a much-lauded tragicomic story of a woman caring for her mentally subnormal sister. After a string of shorts and hit TV films like **Nuts in May** (1975), **Abigail's Party** (1977) and **Meantime** (1983), he returned to the big screen with **High Hopes** (1988), which marked a perfect crystallisation of his previous preoccupations of class differences, political identity and human interaction. **Life is Sweet** (1991), and especially his harrowing and brilliant **Naked** (1993) brought him international acclaim. But it was **Secrets & Lies** (1995), his moving saga of a family's implosion, which took him to a new level of recognition, winning him the Palme d'Or at Cannes and multiple Oscar nominations. **Career Girls** followed in 1997, and then in 1999, he released **Topsy-Turvy**, a startlingly involving portrait of Gilbert and Sullivan, which marked a departure from his trademark intimate ensembles. Another critical triumph, **Topsy-Turvy**, says Leigh, is an "anti-period film". At time of going to press he is at work on **Untitled 2001**, his latest production, which is as usual shrouded in secrecy.

For me the process of film-making is one of discovering what a film is by making it. By a series of flukes and strokes of good fortune, I've always had that freedom, which means that I can privately change direction, pursue and discover things that might hopefully make a more profound and complex piece of work than I might conventionally have made. Obviously my aspiration is to make films which are very precise, organised, well-written and tightly scripted, but the actual depths of the film, the writing and conception, are entangled with the whole, so I always embark without a script. The kind of things which I'm motivated to put on the screen – the way people interact, people in the raw etc. – lend themselves to working in this way. My personal process of distilling things and working out how people will play the characters and how the characters interact is quite sophisticated. Through that process, we arrive at a kind of premise with a ready built-in metaphor before we shoot. At first the specific premise doesn't exist. With **High Hopes**, I had a sense of certain things I felt I wanted to say around the political arena. What I hadn't identified prior to making the

Scene 11	PHOTOGRAPHER'S (Day Int/Ext Monday Week 2) Maurice. Customers. Jane.	
Scene 12	OPTICIAN'S (Day Int Tuesday Week 2) Hortense. Customer/s.	
Scene 13	PHOTOGRAPHER'S (Day Int Wednesday Week 2) Maurice. Customers. Jane.	
Scene 14	HORTENSE'S FLAT (Day/Night Int Thursday Week 2) Hortense. Document. Envelope.	
Scene 15	LETTER-BOX (Day Ext Friday Week 2) Hortense.	

Scene 16	PHOTOGRAPHER'S (Day Int/Ext Saturday Week 2) Maurice. Jane. Customer/s.
Scene 17	WHITEHOUSE WAY (Day Int/Ext Saturday Week 2) Maurice. Monica.
N.B. NO WEEK 3	
Scene 18	HORTENSE'S FLAT (Night Int Monday Week 4) Hortense. Letter.
Scene 19	OPTICIAN'S (Day Int Tuesday Week 4) Hortense. Phone.
Scene 20	WHITEHOUSE WAY (Day/Night Int/Ext Tuesday Week 4) Monica. Maurice.

Scene 51	QUILTER STREET (Day/Night Int/Ext Thursday Week 7) Cynthia. Roxanne.
Scene 52	A RENDEZVOUS (Day/Ext Saturday Week 7) Cynthia. Hortense.
Scene 53	A CAFE (Day/Night Int/Ext Saturday Week 7) Cynthia. Hortense.
Scene 54	STREETS, QUILTER STREET (Night Ext Saturday Week 7) Cynthia. Hortense. Car.
Scene 55	QUILTER STREET (Day Int/Ext Sunday Week 8) Roxanne leaves. Cynthia. Phone.

1   2   3

4

5

(1–8) **Secrets & Lies:** (1–3) Extracts from Leigh's bare-bones shooting script or structure, show that there is literally no dialogue nor even clear storyline available before the cameras start to roll. The rich tableaux of customers in Maurice's photography studio is scenes 13 and 16. (4) The photographer's studio scene and the café scene (7). "All of those people in scenes 13 and 16 came on the day, and we cooked it up on the spot. We planned what the people were going to be in the previous weeks – I knew that Mia Soteriou and the other guy had Greek Cypriot backgrounds and that Alison Steadman would bring the dog and that Angela Curran would bring her kid and so on. That scene was all about getting on a roll and being very creative, yet it's all within the discipline of looking at it from Maurice the photographer's point of view. This scene is one of the few which is entirely improvised on camera."

Secrets & Lies: (6) "There is one scene outside on the patio which is one of two now-famous scenes in that film, which holds up in one shot, the other one being in the café with the two women (7). The former is a scene where there are seven characters at the barbecue, and the reason I shot it in that way was because first of all I knew we were to go indoors (8), where there would be a lot of cutting, and the dynamics would be very much close-up. The scene is a very good example of the relationship between the dynamics of the shot and the narrative function of the moment, because at that point in the story you assume the shit's going to hit the fan. You're watching everybody and you know, and yet they're all just behaving in apparently a socially acceptable way, and so I felt I needed to let it happen so that you could look wherever you wanted and make choices and wonder and expect and anticipate, and within that scene if you listen to what's going on and watch it, it keeps sailing very near the storm."

6

7

8

UNTITLED '98

SC.	DAY	ACTION	LOCATION	D/N	INT/EXT	✓
37	17	Sword.....	GILBERT'S HOUSE	N	Int	X
38	18	"The Mikado" Ko-ko's entrance	SAVOY STAGE	N	Int	X
39	19	G reads to S	SULLIVAN'S FLAT	D/N	Int	X
40	20	G reads to KITTY	GILBERT'S HOUSE	D/N	Int	X
41	21	Grossmith, Barrington, Lely	OYSTER BAR	D	Int	
42	21	CARTE → + LEONORA	CARTE'S OFFICE	D/N	Int	
43	21	Temple, Lely	SAVOY: DR 1	N	Int	
44		G reads to Company	SAVOY: Stage/Aud	D	Int	
45	23	"The Mikado" A Wand. Minister	SAVOY STAGE	N	Int	X
46	24	Sullivan spiel, Louis CLOT	SULLIVAN'S FLAT (?)	N	Int	
47	25	Sullivan rehearsal	Savoy Stage	D	Int	X
48	25	playing with BLOCKS	GILBERT'S HOUSE	N	Int	
49	26	G reh. "Mikado" Act 1	SAVOY STAGE	D	Int	
50	26	Madame Leon, &	SAVOY STAGE	D	Int	
51	27	D reh "Mikado how-de-do"	SAVOY STAGE	D	Int	
52	27	Japanese Visit	SAVOY STAGE/Aud	D	Int	
53	28	"The Mikado" 3 Little maids	SAVOY STAGE	N	Int	X
54	29	G rehearse Mikado: Execution?	SAVOY STAGE/Aud	D	Int	X

(1–6) **Topsy-Turvy**: While shooting, Leigh always wears shirts with pockets, in which to keep one or two cards on which the basic structure of the film is mapped out. "It's my script – I refer to it constantly, and I hate having to carry things around." (1) One of the cards Leigh used for the film. A historical piece about composers Gilbert and Sullivan, **Topsy-Turvy** was nevertheless created, says Leigh, with the "same process" as all his films, "which is to say a huge amount of discussion, improvisation and research, which is always a characteristic. It just happened that there was more research in this case by definition because it drew on history, which it actually deals with to some extent accurately, and therefore deals with people who really existed. Some are complete inventions, like the character that Timothy Spall plays (6, left). That person really existed, but we know very little about him and so that left us free to create his character. Whereas Jim Broadbent's Gilbert and Allan Corduner's Sullivan were carefully researched, in an attempt to bring to life the men as we understand they were." (2) Leigh on the set of **Topsy-Turvy**.

film, but identified very clearly by the process of making it, and what I wanted to say was how difficult it is for us to express what we feel and how difficult it is for us to call ourselves socialists. Another thing on the go with that film was the reaction I had to my Dad having died a couple of years earlier, and coping with an elderly parent. In **Life is Sweet**, I had the notion of the two sisters and I knew I wanted to do something about a family, but it wasn't until we were actually doing it that I thought of the idea of them being twins. During rehearsals, I was working with the actresses, and I suddenly thought we could make them look pretty similar. I also wanted to do something about comfort – therefore food was an idea, but I didn't know how that was going to manifest itself. By the time I got to **Naked**, I knew I wanted to deal with unacceptable sides of male behaviour in relation to women, and also had a vague notion that I wanted to attempt something to do with the coming apocalypse... the end of the century. On **Secrets & Lies**, I wanted to deal with the issue of adoption, because there are some people close to me who have bad adoption-related experiences.

These notions are very fluid and contain unrelated elements, although there are also ongoing preoccupations such as class, or rather the differences between factions in groups and the difference between people who move on, like the upwardly mobile sister in **Meantime** or the brother in **Secrets & Lies**. But at the point of casting, there is absolutely no story. So the first manifest part of the creative process is casting, which is tough. Apart from anything else, you can't do it with any old actor. You have to get character actors who are versatile, have a sense of humour and of society, who can improvise and aren't completely self-absorbed. I spend months casting, and it's a very empirical thing. There'll be all these people in the cast and I won't have any idea who they are going to play. It starts with a very intensive one-to-one with myself and each actor to get a character, and I may only work with two or three people a day. Once that gets going, I have to work in the evenings as well so it's very hard work. It would be economically unviable for everybody to be on the payroll at this stage, so we work out a pyramid system whereby people join in as the weeks go by, and then I schedule them to drop out during the shoot with my option to extend. We have a rigidly fixed budget, so I have to work within those limits.

When we started **Secrets & Lies**, I decided that Timothy Spall and Brenda Blethyn will be a brother and sister, and we just started off by talking about the core of the relationship and the chronology and dynamics of that family. Her kid daughter. His wife. And then, with Brenda, I invented the notion of the girl who was given away and in another rehearsal I invented that other history with Marianne [Jean-Baptiste]. I always ask each actor to come up with an extensive, nay exhaustive, list of real people that he or she has known, and after detailed discussion about these people, I select one or sometimes more than one to use as a starting point for the character. The rehearsals consist of improvisations where the actors are solidly in character, always wearing the costumes, working with a lot of furniture and props. These improvisations are in real time. The actors are under no pressure to be interesting. Their job is to be real and let the character develop in an organic way. When I get to day one of the shoot, I've already been in rehearsal for some time, although this period contains no actual rehearsal of the film itself. During this time, I am not in a position to say what the premise is. The production, costume and make-up designers traditionally stay adjacent and are ready for me to say anything I can to indicate what it might be. Alison Chitty, who designed **Life is Sweet**, **Naked** and **Secrets & Lies**, describes the whole thing as a group of people gathering around a black hole. At this point I am working with each actor in a specific, hands-on way on characterisation, behaviour, language and so on, but on another level, I am making decisions about the basic dramatic premise. I don't talk about anything to anyone at this point as I would be bull-shitting, because nothing is yet crystallisable, but also – and this is the most esoteric area – it's important the actors never know anything except what their characters would know right until the end of the shoot. A lot of people never really find out what they're taking part in until they see the film. It's not about treating actors like idiots. On the contrary, it's because through genuine, organic improvisations, you can engender truthful, spontaneous material – that's what you see on screen.

So that by the time we had shot four-fifths of **Secrets & Lies**, I set up an improvisation in Maurice and Monica's house, and all the characters arrived from different parts of London having stayed in character, and it lasted about ten hours in real time. There was a barbecue; it rained; the truth came out. This sort of master improvisation gives me the raw material from which I then distil the structure. I rehearse a sequence which will then be shot as you see it. At this stage in the film, none of the actors knew any more than their characters did at that point – so, not only did they not know who Hortense was, but we'd shot all the scenes with her, and security was so tight that they weren't allowed to know about them. When we shot Brenda and Marianne coming out of the Odeon Cinema Leicester Square, we checked the cast to make sure nobody would be in Leicester Square on their night off. People enter into the spirit of the thing. It's all about getting the results.

During the rehearsal process, I have to start different kinds of discussions with the crew, in particular the costume designer and make-up artists. At a certain point in **Naked**, I was able to sit down with Dick Pope [the cinematographer] and Alison and talk loosely about this guy on a journey, using words like nocturnal, monochromatic, dark. They got it. Also during this period, the production designer and I will start looking at locations. What we normally do (**Topsy-Turvy** excepted) is to have one or two main locations which are acquired and dressed for the entire shoot which we can start at and always go back to, like the house in **Life is Sweet**, or the main pad in **Naked**. The most interesting thing at this stage is how the shoot is organised given that there's still no script or other locations. At a very late stage in the rehearsal proceedings, I write a scenario, a structure: a simple document telling you no more than where and when a scene takes place e.g. Maurice comes out of house, night interior, monologue. I go away for a couple of days to do it. It's really the only time I have to write the film, bearing in mind that I've already described how we didn't really develop the scene at the end of **Secrets & Lies** until we'd shot three-quarters, or never knew what the end of **Naked** would be until it came to doing it. Nevertheless, I imagine my way through the rhythms and make some decisions that go down on paper. There'll be scenes I am clear I know what they're going to be and scenes I don't. So it will actually say, "Scene 29. Office block. Johnny meets Brian". With that document, the actors have a sense of what the journey means from their point of view, the costume designer knows what each person will wear each day, the production designer can start planning the logistics of locations.

The location is important because you can see plainly from my films that the place has informed the action. In that

(1–4) During **Naked**, Leigh struggled with certain scenes in the dark journey of Johnny (David Thewlis): "Sometimes a scene that looks like it's not going to be pivotal becomes major and vice versa. Arriving at the precise events which would conclude **Naked** was quite complex. Does Johnny stay? Does he take the money? Does he meet her? We were shooting at the house, and every day I would arrive in the morning in my car and drive along this road, with the house at the end of it. Eventually what I was looking at permeated my thick early-morning cranium and I started to see it. I thought this was a fantastic view. And I thought, I know what happens, he walks away. So I asked Dick Pope [the cinematographer] if we could track in the street, and he said that the only way to do it was with Steadicam. It's the only Steadicam shot in any of my films. The shot immediately liberated what actually happened, which was that he walks away and then the film stops and the rest is up to you. He can't go and meet her. He has to walk away. And of course he takes the money. Of course he does. The location gave me the closing image."

3

4

1

2

(1–3) In rehearsals on **Career Girls**, Leigh worked with his actors building through the layers appropriate to the relationship between the two protagonists (played by Katrin Cartlidge and Lynda Steadman). "Traditionally, finally, I arrive at the present, which is more or less the year the film is made, and I drop anchor and tell the story. The rest is in the ether, in the background, in the motivating forces. And it occurred to me mid-rehearsals to actually set half of it in 1986, ten years prior to the year it was being made. I immediately talked to the production designer and costume designer and who does the make-up and Dick Pope about how to make the distinction cinematographically, both in terms of stock and in the way we shot it. Of course I didn't tell the actors for a long time. I even remember Katrin saying what a shame it was we couldn't actually do the 1986 stuff, and I didn't say anything. Finally I told them, and it was a big surprise because these actors are in their early thirties and I was asking them to play people of 20. But they did it." (4) Leigh shooting on location for **Secrets & Lies**.

famous conclusive sequence in **Secrets & Lies**, you know the actual logistics of the house – the patio, the lavatory next to the table, the front door in relation to the bus stop. So we rehearse on the location. If the bus stop hadn't been there, the story would have been different. And that's part of the joy of it, because you create a world you absolutely believe in. Shooting is very hard work on me and the actors. I go in and I think I've got two days for this one scene, but often it's not straightforward, because you have to put everything into context. It's tough because there's no point in trying to start the improvisation until you've got the premise in place. Sometimes it's straightforward because we are coming from a previous scene and it's something we can plug right back into. Other times, you're inventing. It's a combination of what actually happened in the rehearsals, things that may have been talked about and things that never happened at all that I've invented. But of course it's very important conceptually to realise that the only thing of any consequence is shooting the film. Everything that happens prior to that is just preparation.

Very often you'll come to a sequence which is new territory, but what's good is you've got a bunch of actors who absolutely know who they are and they can do it. I work up the scene to the point where it's absolutely structured. They learn it by rehearsal, not by it being written down. Good actors can do that. And what I do in my writer capacity is not just dialogue but subtext; I'll set something up in relation to what I can see. I can only script a scene when I actually see it. That's the only thing that motivates me; I can't do it in an abstract void. When it comes to the actual dialogue, I'm saying, "let's do that or let's swap those around". It's writing through directing. And it can only be done by absolutely understanding not only the actor but the character and the rhythms of the character.

When Dick and I are working out a scene, we'll run it as much as we need to, and – this is where you have to be cheeky – if it takes three hours to work out how to shoot it, everyone has to be patient… though it's usually quicker! Then while he's lighting, unless something is perfect, I will always be off with the actors, refining the dialogue. I don't shoot many takes or a lot of footage because, on the whole, it's so precise. I do on the intimate scenes because I get into the most subtle quests for nuance and accuracy of the moment, but usually the production team and completion guarantors bully me for that – they think I'm wasting footage. I'm not a fan of the indiscriminate use of video playback. I don't look at a screen during the take. I stand next to the camera and do it the old-fashioned way. That way I can concentrate. The operator is seeing the shot, and I am empathising with what's going on. Similarly I won't let actors watch rushes. In my experience if they see themselves perform it affects them greatly. I love post-production though. Apart from anything else, it's when you make the film. Having a good editor is as important to me as other people during the shoot. While we're shooting, he or she gets an assembly on the go and I start thinking about music. The musical values in my films are very important. I like Andrew Dickson, Rachel Portman and Carl Davis – emotional, subjective people who express what they feel in response to a film. That's what music is all about.

One of the things that is so distressing about some reactions to my films is that people talk about me as though I'm playing some sort of deceitful trick, whereby I am merely exploiting the actors and getting them to do all the work which I then take credit for. But we spend months reaching the shooting stage. It's not just a whole lot of improvisations that I then structure in a journalistic way and bang on the screen.

biography

An unstinting innovator, an outspoken *enfant terrible*, a technical genius, a brutal manipulator, Lars von Trier is one of European cinema's most original talents. Dividing the audience like no other contemporary film-maker, von Trier's first film **The Element of Crime** (1984) – made two years after leaving the National Film School of Denmark in Copenhagen – hinted at the boldness of the man.

lars von trier

That kicked off a so-called "Europe" trilogy which continued with **Epidemic** in 1988 and **Europa** in 1991. Each of the three films was technically novel, as was a 1987 TV version of 'Medea', based on a treatment by Carl Theodor Dreyer and his popular 1994 TV miniseries *The Kingdom*. In 1995, von Trier and fellow Danish film-makers Thomas Vinterberg, Soren Kragh-Jacobsen and Kristian Levring established the Dogme 95 manifesto in cinema, to "force the truth out of characters and settings". It required film-makers to shoot on location using only hand-held cameras without using sets, props or lighting. But before Dogme was to produce any movies, von Trier unleashed the emotionally devastating **Breaking the Waves** on an unsuspecting world, kicking off a trilogy of films based around female characters in dire straits. **Breaking the Waves** (1996), followed by his controversial Dogme film **The Idiots** (1998) and **Dancer in the Dark** (2000), a lavish musical tragedy shot, like **The Idiots**, on digital video, established von Trier as a household name to be revered or reviled. He is currently in production on **Dogville**, a US-set drama which will be shot on high-definition.

interview

I wanted to be a director when I was ten. My uncle was a director of documentaries, and I remember being fascinated by the editing tables, which were the fantastic Steenbeck at the time, although I'm not sure I knew what it was all about. When I was 12, I was making small feature-films, which took place in the woods around my house, with the hand-held camera. The most refined thing at the time was I discovered if you used indoor film outdoors, you could get these weird, bluish colours. That was great, and I wanted to know more about that. I used 8mm cameras for eight years before moving on to 16mm. I'm crazy about these Bolex cameras and felt I could do anything with them – expose the film and take it back, do single frames and triple exposure and so on. I tried every technique.

I made **The Element of Crime** when I left film school, with a cinematographer [Tom Elling] and editor [Tomas Gislason] from film school, and we had already done three films together, so the look of the film was more or less already developed. I had this idea that a film should have a specific

directing

(1–5) Von Trier's **Breaking the Waves** – the story of a woman who sacrifices herself for love – was shot on the Isle of Skye in 1995 in a strict Calvinist community. Von Trier had wanted to cast Helena Bonham Carter in the lead role of Bess, but she dropped out and he replaced her with an unknown English stage actress, Emily Watson. Von Trier separated the intense drama into chapters of sorts with glam-rock interludes reflective of the early '70s setting. "I'm sure that when I put that music in, I could have told you exactly what the rationale was for it, but I'm not so sure anymore. I thought that it was a good parallel to the story of Bess if we had something else coming in from the outside to this little isolated place – in this case, glam-rock." (4–5) Von Trier on set with Emily Watson and Stellan Skarsgård.

language and it should not just be in Danish because it was shot in Denmark. For **The Element of Crime**, it was a *film noir*, and it was therefore evident to me that it should be shot in English.

The Element of Crime and **Europa** are extremely precise. We storyboarded everything and edited on the storyboards because we had a lot of ideas at the time about how an image should sew into another image. **The Element of Crime** was incredibly complicated and took three months to draw. Now I hate storyboards. I stopped using them on *The Kingdom*. It's interesting to storyboard and to plan out a film, but from then on you can only go downhill because you can never achieve what you had in mind. That means that on a good day you can get 70 per cent of what you had in mind. If you don't use storyboards, you can reach 100 per cent every day because you are building everything up from zero. I just feel it now when I have my 100 per cent. It's more intuitive, and for me it's a more fulfilling way to work, although maybe that has to do with my development as a person, because I believe that I have always been afraid of losing control and I shouldn't be. If I can train myself not to be afraid of that, then I would be a happier person. When we storyboarded, I controlled everything by drawing. Luckily, I've always been in control in a financial way. It's why we founded Zentropa [von Trier's production company].

On **The Idiots** I started shooting myself, using these small video cameras, and on **Dancer in the Dark**, Robby Müller took care of the lighting and I operated the camera for the whole film. The hand-held camera is a very personal thing. It moves where your interest lies. I think I have said one very wise thing in my life: when I was asked to define the difference in photography betwen a Dogme and non-Dogme film, I said that on a non-Dogme film, you frame, but when you do Dogme, you point. When you look around in life, you point. When you frame, you are interested in the limits of a picture, but when you point, you are interested in content. You know exactly what you've got because you've filmed it yourself. It's very different from looking at a monitor, which I simply don't do anymore. The hand-held camera maintains the actors' freedom and I would like to give them as much freedom as possible, in the sense that if they thought it was good for a scene, they could for example walk from a house to a garden instinctually and I could film all that with the camera. I have to push them to think like this, but most actors I've spoken to like this technique because they're not restricted by keeping marks on the floor. What's more, the video camera allows me to shoot for an hour, which is fantastic, so I can do the same scene over and over again.

On **The Idiots**, I would start by asking the actors how they thought they would like to play the scene or just to do it for me without rehearsals which I would film. Then I could start to see what my 100 per cent would be. I have a technique where I like to play the scene in many different ways and then cut them together afterwards. You can actually get what I call a psychological time-cut this way. A time cut of course is cutting from a man being on the first step of a staircase to him being on the last step. You accept that in the film there is nothing interesting happening on the stairs in-between. I first used psychological time-cuts on *The Kingdom*. I now use it commonly by asking the actors to do the scene completely differently a few times. You could look at a scene as sad, but you could also look at it as having happy things in it. I would shoot first with the sad way in mind and then from the happier

1

(1–4) **Dancer in the Dark**: (1–3) Von Trier was never going to be conventional in his filming of the musical numbers, which he shot using up to 100 carefully-positioned fixed cameras. "The musical is something in which you execute a number by moving the camera to the music. You can't go wrong. That's how it is. Because traditionally musicals are shot with moving cameras and that has been taken to extremes by pop videos, I didn't want to do it like that because it would become too much of a pastiche. I wanted a fresher look. Then I tried to think what the most difficult thing I could do would be, and that was to have fixed images, so I went with that. I sat down with my former editor Tomas Gislason and we concluded that there would be something to gain from having a live performance quality to it. That was the original plan: to have the actors sing and dance only once and have enough cameras running to cover the whole thing as if it were a performance. Björk also had the idea that she wanted to sing live, which is fantastic, and she could really do it. In the end, we didn't really have the money and technique to do it, so the musical numbers are actually cut from more than one take." Von Trier was ultimately not entirely content with the experiment, saying that 100 cameras were not enough. Because the performers were not being shot by any one camera, they would cross in the sights of each camera randomly. "That was what we were after, but for it to work you need about 1,000 or 2,000 cameras. I believe that the scenes are cut too fast, but that's because of the material we had to work with. The intentions were that we would film a live event. I still believe there was something to that."

2

3

THE SELMA MANIFESTO

Selma comes from the east. She loves musicals. Her life is hard, but she can survive because she has a secret. When things get too rough she can pretend that she is in a musical … just for a minute or two. All the joy that life cannot give her there. Joy is not living … joy is there so we can stand life. The joy that she can produce from within her is her spark of happiness.

Selma loves The Sound of Music along with all the other great song and dance films. And she is the one who is going to star in the very same The Sound of Music in an amateur production … at the same time as she is about to achieve her greatest goal in life. It seems that for Selma, dream and reality are converging at last.

So popular music and the great musicals are all there on the shelves of her brain. But she is more than a dreamer! She is a lover of all life! She can cherish the wonder of every little detail of her (pretty hostile) world. And she can see the details … all of them. Funny things that only she sees or hears. She is a true observer … with a photographic memory. And it is this double sidedness that makes her an artist: her love and excitement for the artificial world of music, song and dance, and her compassionate fascination with real life … her humanity. Her own work of art is the little gems of musicals that she retreats to in hours of need … fragments of Selma's musical … it is unlike any other musical……it is the clash between all the snatches of melody, tunes, sounds, instruments, text and dance that she ever heard in the cinema, and true life with all the same elements that she—with her gift—is able to find there.

It is not just escapism …..it is far more….it is art! It derives from a true inner need to play with life and put it into her own private world.

A situation can be painful beyond words, but it can always be used for the creation of yet another little outbreak of Selma's art. Be put into the little world that she controls.

About the film:

To tell Selma's story the film must embody her world. All the scenes that do not include her musical fantasies must be as realistic a possible in terms of the acting, sets, etc. Because the scenes from Selma's normal life are the input that she uses in her musicals…and that has to be true to life. What she sees in the cinema is flawless….painless….and this is where real life is the opposite…..here it is the flaws and the pain that make it shine. The indications of humanity….of nature…..of life!

So the events of the plot will partly be the best, most controlled beauty of music, scored according to unequivocal systems—juxtaposed with all the flaws and clumsy mistakes of reality. These are the two orchestras that will play together.

And this is the principle of Selma's musicals that we will have to show. Punk is the word I would like to emphasise: as I see it, punk is a clash between tradition and nature. It is not destructive…it is celebratory, for it goes back to basics….by confronting the system with a modern and therefore truer view of life….forcing life into what has grown stale….by violence. This might be the only form of violence Selma concurs with?

Music:

Any musical elements that contain instruments and tunes will come from the musicals she loves. They may be fragments incorporated into other systems….or instrumental sounds used differently. Selma loves the cheapest musical effects. The riffs and all the other clichés…..and she uses them far beyond any good taste…..but these things are combined with the sounds of life, and there she is far from banal. She loves the basic sounds of living things….hands, feet, voices etc….(the sighs arising out of hard work?)….the noise of machines and things mechanical….the sounds of nature…..and mostly the little sounds of mistakes…. the clicking of a piece of the floor that has a defect, maybe. Her music is the celebration of a dream on one the one hand, and of life on the other. In the music she uses her situation in order to create. Mostly to use it positively…but a few times to sing her pain out, too ….What is very important is that the artificial side should still sound artificial…..we have to know where things

(4) To begin a dialogue with the creative talent on **Dancer in the Dark**, von Trier wrote a booklet called 'The Selma Manifesto' and sent it to them. "It talked about the characters and what the different parts of the film were and encouraged their input. Otherwise why would you hire Björk and not give her creative freedom? The same with the choreographer Vincent Harrison. I could have got a computer to do it." The personal differences between von Trier and Björk on the set of **Dancer in the Dark** are now semi-legendary. "She wouldn't tell you, but she does hate me… But ultimately it doesn't matter. It's history, and it wasn't a professional thing, it was on a personal level. It's a pity if you don't hit it off and you want to be nice and civilised to people, and we couldn't achieve that. It is somewhat irritating if you have those problems with a collaborator for three years of your life, it gives you a scar. Having said that, just from the readings Björk was fantastic. She is good, there's no question about it."

way. When you cut these different moods together, it gives the scene a feeling of life. Maybe it's not very realistic, but then again the psychology an actor forms for himself may not be very realistic anyway. It's fun to shoot this way because it's a kind of game. I also ask the actors to redo scenes but not using any of the words they've just used. They are little games which pump life into the scenes. Björk, for example, was extremely good at this in **Dancer in the Dark**. She was feeling things very deeply, but she was also able to change, and the good thing when you film her is that, as long as you hold her hand and tell her what to do, you know she will listen and do whatever you want.

On **Breaking the Waves**, we had a very good camera operator, but he was very conscious of framing all the time. In the end, I had to cheat him by telling him to pan to Emily Watson on the right, and when he moved to the right he'd realise she was on the left so he'd have to quickly move to the left. Another revelation on *The Kingdom* was something we copied from the US TV series *Homicide*, which was to throw away access rules. Although it since calmed down, *Homicide* started off by cutting wildly from one thing to another. Normally you would only film the interaction or access between two people on one side, otherwise the audience would get confused if there was an access jump. Or so we were told in film school. 99.9 per cent of films today still use these rules, but the most interesting thing is that the audience don't miss it when it's not used.

I have learned to write the script as simply as possible because if you want actors to improvise, it shouldn't be too sophisticated. It's when you film that you put on all the layers or camouflage or life or whatever you want to call it. There are

some acting scenes early in **Dancer in the Dark** which I really like, before you know what it's all about. There's one where the son is given a bike, which came out very lively and the actors really used their freedom; I also very much liked the confession scene where Björk talks to David Morse about going blind and they discuss musicals.

I've worked with some difficult actors in my time. I've also had the privilege of working with some amazing first-time actors. For Emily Watson on **Breaking the Waves**, she knew that she had to surrender to the project – indeed, she didn't have much of a choice – because she didn't know so much then about what she could or couldn't do. Part of the advantage also with Björk was that she didn't know her own strength yet. You just have to let these talents live. I'm sure on their second film, actors think they know what their strengths are, but I like it more when they have to trust me. When an actor is going into any European film, they have to talk to the director and decide if they will go with his film or not, because the only thing I can show is what I have done before, and from those films they can see that I'm serious. It's like going on a plane – you have to trust the pilot.

With some of these roles for women, it's a question of finding actors who want to live it a little, and that was what Björk was doing and Emily, and also Bodil Jørgensen [in **The Idiots**], who is a very good actor as well. I also, of course, work with some very experienced actors. Stellan Skarsgård has this quality which I think few actors possess, which is that he supports very well. He supported Emily extremely well and made her better by his presence. A lot of actors would do the opposite. David Morse also has that quality.

4

5

(5) Storyboard from **Europa**, starring Jean-Marc Barr (4). Inspired by the look of Charles Laughton's **The Night of the Hunter**, **Europa** was shot using the old-fashioned technique of back and front projection. The film was shot on a sound stage and then background footage was projected behind the actors. "It was often technical and the actors had to be very precise, so it wasn't a spontaneous film to make. It was very theatrical. We had a fantastic shot of a model train, which ended up inside a compartment of the train where Udo Kier had a long monologue. We filmed for a whole day, and Udo had to stand on a little trolley which moved and made him look like he was on a moving train. But every time the camera got to him, we cut. He was getting very frustrated, and then when we did get to him, he forgot his lines. It didn't help when I joked that we should have got Max von Sydow instead." (1–3) Storyboards from **The Element of Crime**.

1

2

3

(1–4) Von Trier's first film made under the Dogme manifesto was **The Idiots**, which he wrote in just four days. The story of a commune of young men and women who pretend that they are mentally handicapped in order to win charitable donations, **The Idiots** featured an explicit orgy scene which von Trier directed in the nude in order to make the actors feel more at ease. "It was great to have the freedom of the good old days, you know, running around naked." In the US however, censors refused to allow the erect penis shots from the orgy. "I came up with the idea of having these rectangular boxes so that you could get a clue to the excitement of the characters by how big was the size and angle of the box."

4

I didn't conceive the last three films as a trilogy, but the good thing about trilogies is that you can do the same thing over and over as well as putting different angles on the subject. **Dancer in the Dark** was just **Breaking the Waves** as a musical more or less. **Breaking the Waves** was extremely simple to write. I was inspired by a book for children I had when I was a child, called 'The Gold Heart', about a little girl who went out into the forest and gave away all that she had to the starving animals. I found this "giving away" thing quite interesting. I started **Breaking the Waves** with the tricky combinations of religion and sex, and was experimenting with them like you would in a chemistry set. I combined melodrama and musical in **Dancer**. On **The Idiots** the combination was the mentally handicapped and penetration.

I like the genre of melodrama – my parents were socialists, and melodrama was an opium for the people, so of course, because it was forbidden to me, I got interested in it when I was older. I tend to take genres a little further than they normally go. This has been my technique – to take an idea and go a little further than sensible people. All the stories have been about idealists who have come to some point where reality and ideas collide. Some people call me sadistic, but I'm allowed to do that to my characters aren't I? Maybe I do get pleasure out of making them suffer, but if you're a real sadist, that's a form of love also. It depends how you define it.

Dramatic things don't happen in editing. I pretty much know what the material is and you've got to find out how you're going to use it. Of course the first edit is always too long. **Breaking the Waves** was about five hours of film stock, and you cut that down, feel you've gone too far, put a little bit back in and so on. I don't like films to be too short. I think that a film should always be a little too long. If I think of all the films I like, they are all a bit too long. All the Fellini films, for example, go on forever. It's like listening to Wagner. In the end it's reassuring because you know they're there.

Dogme 95 started when I sat down to think about what I didn't want to spend my time on in the light of what I spent my time on before. I used to spend hours and hours on how the colours of a film should look. Well, I thought, why not make a rule which says you are not allowed to care about that. Other things, like lighting, sprang from that. And so you focus on working with the actors and not waiting for three hours because somebody has to put up the lights or tracks. I'm not saying it should be done like that all the time, but it reflects what most directors and actors want to do.

The formats which the Dogme films tended to use was digital video, which meant that people in poor countries suddenly felt that they could make films. That was not the intention, but it is a fantastic side result. If they see our films and see that they look like shit and think that they too, therefore, can make films, that's fine with me. I know that a lot of shitty films will come out of the new technology, but if just one or two great ones emerge because of it, then that's a gift. I think the most damaging thing you can do is say it's difficult to make films, and that's what people told me all the time when I started. What's the point in saying this? If you have some knowledge about something, you should share it. Don't take it with you to the grave.

biography

Although his debut film **sex, lies, and videotape** (1989) was adopted as the mascot for America's vibrant new independent movement of the early '90s, director Steven Soderbergh has found his greatest success recently at the heart of Hollywood's studio system. Working with box-office stars such as Julia Roberts and Michael Douglas, he single-handedly re-injected a dose of realism and intelligence into

steven soderbergh

mainstream pictures with both **Erin Brockovich** and **Traffic** in 2000. His ambitious fusion of traditional storytelling skill, kinetic visual styles and expertly naturalistic approach in both, won him a heap of accolades and success, and elevated him to the top of the Hollywood pile. It contrasted starkly with his struggle to find audiences for a decade after **sex, lies**, which won the audience award at the Sundance Film Festival and the Palme d'Or at Cannes in 1989. The mixed success of **Kafka** (1991), **King of the Hill** (1993) and **The Underneath** (1995) brought him to a professional turning point which coincided with a personal malaise. In response, he made the intensely personal no-budget experiment **Schizopolis** (1996), followed by a film of the Spalding Gray monologue **Gray's Anatomy** (1997). Artistically renewed, Soderbergh took on **Out of Sight**, a critically adored thriller, in 1998, and then the lower-budget revenge drama **The Limey** in 1999, before his banner year 2000. His star-studded remake of **Ocean's 11** was released in late 2001, and he is currently at work on the comedy **How to Survive a Hotel Room Fire.**

interview

I didn't wonder who made movies until I saw **Jaws** when I was 12. I was so terrified by it that I bought 'The Jaws Log' [a diary of shooting the film] – two copies actually, one of which I ripped apart highlighting and re-reading. But I realise now that, while watching other movies is a given, the biggest influence on my aesthetic is the people that I started making films with. I had a mentor of sorts called Michael McCallum, a documentary film-maker who taught classes at Louisiana State University. When I was at high school, I used to hang out in his classes for four years or so. His ideas about how you work and how you behave towards other people were the biggest influence of all on me. He had definitive ideas about standards of quality and artistic integrity which have so much to do with how I work on set today. I learned from him that there's a way to get what you want without diminishing people. Similarly, you (the director) are the audience. Anything you can follow, they can follow, and you must never take the attitude that they are less than you. On the one hand, I don't think about the audience when I'm making a film. You're the dog and they're the tail, and you need always to keep that in

1

2

(1–4) Soderbergh says he has always had "a European approach to character and style, and it isn't until recently that that blend seems to be satisfying to people." **Erin Brockovich** was the film which reversed the trend: Soderbergh made a traditional woman-against-the-system story into something uniquely his own with the assistance of a giant movie-star in an uncharacteristically unglamourous role (1). "If **Erin** had tanked, you could lay out all the reasons why. It's a terrible title, it's not based on anything you've heard of before, there's no hit song, sequel potential or merchandising, none of the things you have to put across in a movie these days. Fortunately it did work and you can look at the reasons why, most of them paling in comparison to Julia Roberts." Soderbergh downplays his own mark, notably an assertive avoidance of clichéd "movie moments" on the film. For example, Soderbergh and his producers were unhappy with the ending of **Erin**, especially after the first test-screening. "The end wasn't working the way it should have. Some said it was because it didn't have that raised-fist courtroom moment, but I felt there was an emotional beat missing between Julia and Albert Finney (2) – the fact that after they had won the case, you never see them together again. That was what was missing, so Richard La Gravanese wrote this great scene for the two of them."

3

4

mind, but I try to be sensitive when I'm pushing things too far – and that can be in any number of directions – as to how far I can go before I start to lose people. In the case of **The Limey** for example, it was how deconstructed I could get. Then again, I assume that the audience are me and that if I follow my gut about what I like to see, then I'll be OK. You need to temper that with the fact that I've only made three films (**sex, lies, and videotape**, **Erin Brockovich** and **Traffic**) that have made a return on their investment!

When I started, I used to do a lot of rehearsal with actors and now I hardly do any at all. The first four films are really hard for me to watch these days. They're so controlled and formal in their aesthetic in a way that I really reject now. I sort of threw that out and started over again. Fortunately **sex, lies,** had the kind of response that bought me a lot of mistakes, which I took advantage of. As disappointed as I am in the result, I definitely picked the right time to make **Kafka**. The time to risk failure is when you're at your peak. I'm glad I made **The Underneath** in that it pushed me into a very intense period of self-analysis. The ones that don't work are often more important because you know why something doesn't work and you often don't know why something does. I sat on the set of that film, wondering whether I wanted to continue directing. That's how adrift I was. But towards the end of the shoot, I'd come up with a plan: to buy some second-hand gear and make a movie for nothing. While we were in post, I started writing and collecting this equipment and getting **Schizopolis** off the ground. It was essentially financed by Universal, who pre-bought domestic video rights on the understanding that when it was finished I would re-purchase those rights back. It was like my second first film. It was designed to cleanse my palette, and it has informed

everything that has come since. That and **Gray's Anatomy** showed my growing interest in visual abstraction; the latter was shot by Elliot Davis, who shot **Out of Sight**, and you can see a lot of that film in its approach to framing and colour.

If you saw me on set, you'd think I didn't really direct that much. I feel that my job is to create this series of funnels in descending order that lead actors to a place where they're going to give the performance that's best for the movie. It's like a series of hoops you're making sure they go through, which they're not entirely aware of because they are lined with velvet. Very quietly I am leading them to this place where I want them to end up. That works through having contact with the actors before we start shooting, through the way I speak to them as we shoot and the way I run the set. On **sex, lies**, we did a week's worth of rehearsals just running the scenes and talking before shooting. Now all I do is just talk and get everyone out for a couple of dinners, and we end up talking about everything but the movie. At this point, I'm trying to find out how they want to be related to. So when we get to shoot, it's less about control and more about controlled spontaneity. On **Erin**, we had a couple of meetings when I asked if there were any big speed bumps they were running into, but the most important period was the night Julia, Albert, Aaron Eckhart and I went to a restaurant and had a great long dinner and lots of wine. We came away with a really good sense of each other and all liked each other, and that's half the game. In the end, you and the actors have the same objectives. The problems and goals are the same whether it's **Schizopolis** or **Traffic**. And when a movie is made on a bigger scale, like **Traffic**, I have to trick myself creatively into thinking I'm making **Schizopolis**, so that I'm prepared to do anything I think is right in the moment, and not think I

1

(1, 3–7) Iconic British '60s star Terence Stamp was the key for Soderbergh to make his 1999 L.A.-set drama **The Limey**. "I don't think we would have made the movie without him. We built it around him, and Peter Fonda of course (3). Fortunately I'd spoken to him before we pulled the trigger on reworking the script, but it really only worked with the combination of who he is, what his screen persona is and what kind of baggage he has." Soderbergh also used footage of Stamp when he was a young man in Ken Loach's 1967 classic **Poor Cow**, as flashbacks for when Stamp's character was younger (2). "There were months of legal wrangling, since the rights were split, and we didn't get it sorted out until well into the editing phase. When we had it nailed down, I met with Loach and asked whether he was cool with it, and he said fine. It must be weird as a film-maker to get that kind of request." (6) Soderbergh with Stamp on the set of **The Limey**.

2

3

4

5

6

7

can't do that because it's a big movie with movie stars. Each actor I've worked with has fallen into the aesthetic without a peep. There is a very positive atmosphere on my sets. People don't lose focus. It's very low-key and efficient. I know Michael Douglas liked it because we moved so fast. He spent most of his days acting, that's what actors like to do.

99 per cent of **Traffic** was shot on hand-held camera. There are only three shots that weren't. I think I will continue to D.P. my films. After **Traffic**, it will be really hard to go back. It would be like inserting someone into your place. I enjoy doing it and we move more quickly, but principally it gives me this feeling of intimacy, not only with the actors but also the film. For some directors, that's neither possible nor appropriate. I'm not saying everybody should do it, but it reached a point for me where I had to. It was a lengthy process over many years, starting with the fact that I shot my own short films. I was trained as a stills photographer in high school and I was the cinematographer on **Schizopolis** – a sort of dry-run pseudo-Dogme movie. I've always watched my cinematographers very closely, and I was frustrated occasionally by the fact that their idea of what was enough was never in sync with mine. That said, as satisfying as I find it to shoot as well, I was unprepared for how relentless it is. You cannot leave the set for 60 seconds. I'd underestimated the value of saying to Ed Lachman or somebody, "how long?". And he'd say 15 minutes, and I'd go off and clear my head. One of the reasons I think I've been able to work so steadily in the last few years is that I've developed a better sense of where and at what point to invest energy. If you're very precise about where you go in and hit something hard, it will take its own course. Because I have the kind of people around me who know how I work and what I like, I can do that

intense look at something and focus on something else while that gets going. One of those areas of concentration is working with the writer, and that means literally holing up in a room with them and not leaving until we get a draft. We lock ourselves in a hotel room and nobody knows where we are so the phone can't ring, and we don't leave until we have the new draft. That usually takes about three or four days. That's an example of a strategic burst of undiluted attention that ends up having a huge pay-off. What I've realised is that as you learn more, the process ought to and does get easier. We had so much fun making **Erin** that I became convinced it couldn't work commercially. Part of me believed that you should have a bad time for it to be good! Now that the process is becoming easier, I realise I have to find material which pushes me harder or vexes me on some level and keeps me alert. That's why I wanted to do **Ocean's 11**, because it scared me. I really wanted to do it, but I was not sure that I could.

I tend to want to underplay things in my films and find oblique ways to do things that don't hit the audience over the head. I avoid that sort of grandstanding that you see in a lot of films. That doesn't mean the goal isn't the same as for other movies. But I want to find ways of getting there that are slightly circular. **Erin** is a genre movie really, a **Rocky**-type movie, so you're trying to satisfy the expectations of that genre yet find a way to disguise a lot of the signposts and pillars that you know go into any genre film – do a little misdirection so that people don't feel like they see it coming. Every movie is a trick, a conceit, even a documentary is a conceit. As a film-maker, you're trying to suspend that disbelief for as long as you can and get people away from being aware that they're watching a movie. They come into the theatre wanting to disbelieve, wanting to give themselves over to the world of the

1

2

(1–5) **Traffic**: The film had 110 speaking parts and was shot in cities across the Americas. "It's amazing how many movies don't pay attention to the geography in a film – letting the audience know where they are. I've now become obsessed with panning people into places or panning off something and picking up on something else. I've just become very enamoured of shots that show you the whole space of a scene." (3) Benicio del Toro, who won an Oscar for Best Supporting Actor for his performance in the film.

3

4

5

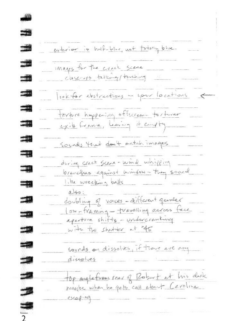

1

remember to ask the basic questions when staging/preparing to shoot:
a) do we need to see the faces of the characters involved?
b) if you had to stage the scene without words, how would you do it?
c) whose scene is it, ultimately?
d) what has come before this and what will come after? Is there an interesting transition to be had?
e) lens length — are we trying to isolate or compress a character in their environment? Should they appear alone in frame or should there always be someone else with them? 50mm+ always feels more real
f) camera speed — is an off-sync speed appropriate here?

be careful with the ASA 800 — I feel sometimes it can be a little soft — although it may have been the Cooke lenses (it was, based on tests @ 3/1)

a full stop push is never a full stop

experiment with pushing two stops (use 500 and 800)

2

exterior is half-blue, not totally blue.

images for the crack scene
closeups, talking/touching

look for abstractions on your locations ←

torture happening offscreen - torturer exits frame, leaving it empty

sounds that don't match images

during crack scene - wind whipping branches against window - they sound like wrecking balls
also:
doubling of voices - different gender
low-framing - travelling across face
aperture shifts - undercranking with the shutter at 45

sounds on dissolves, if there are any dissolves

top angle from rear of Robert at his desk maybe when he gets call about Carolina escaping

3

CU of Robert. Then cut to WS of Robert and ... Pan left to end in similar composition except now ... the lawyer, etc. Then back to tight CU of Robert for the end.

Letters stuck together, separated by colors?
Mexico City, Mexico   La Jolla, California
Columbus, Ohio   Tijuana, Mexico

Slow-motion shot during ...

Short CU reactions of Gordon when Ray dies in the car explosion.

High shot from the corner of the room.

Robert Webber as an example of ...

No player in baseball gets more props than someone who ... It's the equivalent of big glasses and great reviews; the fans love it because

5

6

(1–8) In **Traffic**, Soderbergh – operating the camera under the pseudonym of Peter Andrews – opted to give each of his three storylines a different on-screen hue. "It was to make the audience feel comfortable so they didn't have to think about where they were. (5) For Mexico, I used a tobacco filter number 2, which is a pretty heavy filter, with a 45-degree shutter on the camera, except when we were indoors when I went to a 68-degree because it eats up so much light. We were overexposing significantly, desaturating during a digital step and then taking everything through an ectochrome step in the printing stage. It gives it a suede, blown-out, really high-contrast look. (6) On the east-coast scenes, we didn't use an 85-degree filter, just shooting Tungsten stock all the time, and in San Diego (8), we used a pro-mist 1 filter all the time and usually flashing ten per cent (re-exposing the film before it's developed to white light), which was a trial and error thing. I reshot a lot of the San Diego stuff. Part of the problem with flashing ten per cent is that what you see through the camera bears no relation to what you're going to get. If I was shooting Don Cheadle in front of a window, I couldn't see a thing. The meter tells me he's there, but I have to hold my breath until the dailies come back and then he's there. But it's such an arresting look when it works." (5) Soderbergh with leading man Michael Douglas on location for **Traffic**.

7

(1–4) Extracts from the notebook Soderbergh took on the set of **Traffic**. Starting during **Schizopolis**, Soderbergh began using notebooks as a way of reminding himself of certain ideas during the shoot. "The notebooks are just notes, ideas – remember this, don't forget that – checklists asking myself certain questions when I'm blocking a scene, do I need to see who's talking all the time, is there a way to get an Antonioni thing going in that scene, etc. I keep them because I'm not going to get to do the scene again and I might forget things. When I'm shooting, I also read the script at least once a week, maybe twice, in full. I don't know how many times I've shot a scene and then come to realise that what I thought the scene was about in context was not really. Shooting a movie is like trying to build a house of cards on the deck of a speeding boat. You just can't keep it all on line all the time, and you need moments where you back off and remember the movie that you were thinking about six months ago. When I'm editing, I take a tape of the film home and watch it beginning to end two or three times a week and force myself to sit through it. That way, you get sick of it and you get very ruthless about losing scenes. You know that, when you reach a scene that you're dreading sitting through again, it needs to be dealt with. There's a reason that you're dreading it. You become your worst audience."

4

73

steven soderbergh

8

3

directing

1   2

4

5

(1–5) Soderbergh recalls how particular he was when shooting the famous sexually charged scenes in bar, lift and bedroom between George Clooney and Jennifer Lopez in **Out of Sight**. "I shot a ton of material because the scene is about accidents and finding visual connections that only come about through repetition. Nobody was quite sure what I was doing, because the script was written with a third of the dialogue taking place in the lounge, a third in an elevator and a third in the bedroom. Then they [the characters] got it on. I decided that there was no way I would do it like that, so the day before we shot I let everyone know that I was shooting all the dialogue in the lounge, and then we would do the scene in the bedroom without dialogue. I told them that when I cut them together, they would understand. But I kept grinding and grinding and changing lens sizes and doing take after take. I know the actors and Anne Coates, the film's editor, were wondering what I was up to. Elliot Davis, the cinematographer, did a great job with lighting the set and the trans-light and the snow. It felt exactly the way I wanted it to feel – cold outside and warm inside. She's there alone having a drink, and he shows up and she sees his reflection. You know you want that moment to happen to you." (1, 4, 5) Soderbergh with leading actors and behind camera.

film, and what you've got to do is make sure that you're not having points taken away for making mistakes. That bursts the bubble to some extent. I'm always looking for ways to abstract certain kinds of experiences in a movie. In **Out of Sight**, I wanted to bring the audience further into the emotional world the characters inhabited. The freeze frames in that film were always in my head before we shot. It was my way of telling the audience to remember something because the film was told out of sequence. Also where "Snoopy" Miller takes Glenn into the house and they kill these people. That's an abstract sequence, because literalising would've taken the audience out of the movie instead of pulling them further in.

Right now, I'm pursuing a run-and-gun aesthetic. I didn't realise until after the movie was over how long I spent anti-composing in **Traffic**. As a director, your eye is trained to find order and symmetry in things you look at, and I didn't want that at any point in **Traffic**. It's like having a stroke and learning how to speak again. You have to undo everything. The only time I ever had trouble was in scenes where it seemed the only way to shoot it was the normal way, where everything was properly framed. I wanted to find a place for the camera to end up if somebody said we were going right now and I hadn't had the time to find the right place. Sometimes I wouldn't tell B camera what was going to happen. It was great working with Ed on **The Limey** because he's a great run-and-gun cameraman, and I wanted it to be more immediate after **Out of Sight**, which was very polished. I refined the style more with **Erin**, which for a movie of that type with a big star in it, you'd be stunned how little we lit.

When the gaffer and I enter a space where we're planning to shoot, the first question we ask is how it looks in its natural state. Then we ask if we can shoot it as it is, and if not, what do we need to do to make it look the way it looks to us. Essentially what I try to do is set up circumstances in which it's really hard for you to lie, and part of that is having the camera on your shoulder. If I'm four feet away with the camera on my shoulder, the actor is forced to have the same striving for truth. You live for those moments which feel like life, even in something like **Ocean's 11**. It can be the way somebody feels about something that's happened or the way they look at somebody, or their response to something or a gesture – anything in which a reasonable facsimile of life can take place and the audience recognises it. If you take any story and apply a dose of life to it, it will be interesting.

When we were getting ready for **Erin** and even more so for **Traffic**, I studied the films of Ken Loach: how he framed and staged things; what length of lens; how he used foreground; how he used eye lines to create the impression that this is going on in front of you. I tried to deconstruct it a bit because he's so good at that sense of something happening in front of you. I think **Traffic** works for people because it looks and feels like it's going on right in front of you, and that means shooting available light with hand-held cameras. The reason I'm drawn to this approach is that I feel that if you are going to do something that is lifelike, then it will be inherently self-renewing because life changes, and so if you keep to the idea of trying to capture life as it happens, then your talent won't desert you, whereas with any other style, you know you'll run to a dead end. I'm lucky in that I'm not one of those visionary people whose aesthetic has altered the landscape, like Lynch, Scorsese or Altman. I don't have to worry about my aesthetic being stolen and used in other movies. While I feel lighter on my feet, I want to be as prolific as I physically can be.

biography

Born in New Zealand, Jane Campion attended art school in Sydney, Australia, majoring in painting and sculpture. She made her first Super-8 short film **Tissues** in 1980, subsequently attending the Australian Film TV and Radio School, where she completed three well-regarded shorts: **Peel** (1982); **Passionless Moments** (1984); and her thesis film, **A Girl's Own Story** (1984). She scored immediate success

jane campion

interview

with her first feature **Sweetie** in 1989, a stylised and well-observed social comedy, but it was the film version of a TV miniseries, *An Angel at My Table* (1990), which launched her on the international radar. Telling the painful life story of novelist Janet Frame, **An Angel at My Table** highlighted Campion's visual expressiveness and her skill in eliciting soul-baring performances from her actors. However, the film's achievements were to be surpassed by Campion's third film, **The Piano** (1993), which blended her artist's command of imagery with a keen sense of storytelling. A towering commercial and critical success, **The Piano** won Campion the Palme d'Or at Cannes, making her the first and so far only woman to win it. Her opulent and bold adaptation of Henry James' 'The Portrait of a Lady' in 1996 and **Holy Smoke** (1999), co-written with her sister Anna Campion, again revolved around complex female lead-characters beautifully realised by Nicole Kidman and Kate Winslet respectively. Campion is currently at work on a film of Susanna Moore's novel 'In the Cut' – the story of a creative writing teacher in an affair with a New York detective.

I remember seeing **Belle de Jour** with my mother when I was in bobby socks and, while I felt that I was seeing something way beyond my maturity, it made me want to stretch my understanding. That film, **Performance** and **Women in Love** were seminal movies for me. At university I didn't think about movies much. I went to see the usual pap that everyone sees, and didn't think cinema had any meaning for my life. Then in my early twenties when I was in London, I went to see art cinema at the same time as I was starting to ask questions like, what the fuck is this life about? And I felt that films like Wim Wenders' **The Goalkeeper's Fear of the Penalty Kick** and **Kings of the Road**, or Nic Roeg's **Don't Look Now** and **Bad Timing**, and also Bergman's **Persona**, were speaking directly into my experience. I felt that they were the most intimate experiences I'd ever had. Soon I couldn't see enough film and felt that there was no other medium as modern or fresh, exciting or deeply personal. For example, something like **The Conformist** had such mystery and romance and sensuality in it that I was quite happy not to fully understand it but live with it like a poem in

1

2

3

4

5   6

7

(1–7) Campion's most recent film **Holy Smoke** dealt with a young woman (played by Kate Winslet) caught up in a religious cult while searching for answers about her life in India. Her concerned family hire a top "deprogrammer" (Harvey Keitel) to return her to her senses but – and therein lies the crux of the film – a battle of wills develops between the two. "It shows an incredible time in a young woman's life, when she has this goddess thing in her and she's fearless. At that age, these girl-women haven't really experienced pain and they're kind of ruthless. You have no limits with what you can do. In Harvey's character, she's met by somebody who will see her through it and go through it with her. In the end, she owes him more respect than all these people around her."

(Long lens)
dangerous
be so, beside
or two.

sc 7
must look
but not
a dunking

FLORA –
sick now
or white
being carried
seamen roughly wipes face.

Follow Ada's face or
move to FLORA. TRY at SM.

important to find
good faces for
seamen
good variety
one black
man.

– Ada's dress

from inside boat looking at
waiting hands

confusion – danger – shock

1

sc 9

Possibly much wider

Long lens pan.
OR Better track + pan on rubber
wheeled beach
buggy

schooner
out of ...

washing off pale
from shoulder

seaman flame wipe

track
on with men   to
to reveal → FLORA Puking
or much
closer

2

Sc 13

DUSK

whole bones?

BONES TO PICK
UP SHELL

← TRACK PAST
WHOLE BONES OR
AND OTHER REPTILE

3

(1–3) Storyboards for the opening sequences in **The Piano**, when Ada and her daughter arrive in New Zealand, which were shot on the vast beach at Kare Kare. Campion, who says that the country's bush landscape itself was a lead character in the film, got the idea to have the two carried on the shoulders of Maoris from ship to shore, from a painting on the cover of a book written by Alison Drummond entitled 'Married and Gone to New Zealand'. But shooting the breathtaking scenes turned out to be a problem. "Kare Kare is such a big beach. I was panicking. It was taking us so long to get around that we started to use helicopters to get from one end of the beach to the other. When we finally settled on a spot, we then had to tackle the different tides and weather. You couldn't talk to anyone because you couldn't hear it was blowing so much. One day there was no beach, there was a king tide right up to the dunes, but we found a way of making it dangerous and exciting in the end. It's all about being flexible. Stuart Dryburgh [the cinematographer] is really a cowboy in that respect, and it's great. He's very strong and plain-speaking, which I like. At first I was quite offended by him, but then I found out he didn't take offence at anything. There's no moodiness or sulking with him which you sometimes feel between creative people."

my head. Even then, it never occurred to me to make films. I was just receiving gifts from these film-makers which could help me handle life.

When I went to art school, I started to understand the meaning of having a vision. When I started going to film festivals, I decided that the greatest achievement of my life would be to have my own short animated film screened at the Sydney Film Festival. So I started to make short films at art school and eventually taught myself to use the school Super-8 camera myself. I just kept a chapter ahead of the manual while I made this little short film called **Tissues**, which was a big hit at the school. After that, I was obsessed by wanting to be in the film industry some way or another, and was accepted at the film school the following year.

When I made **Tissues**, I didn't know that there was such a thing as a wide shot or a long shot. I was very naïve. Finally somebody who had been at the BFI (British Film Institute) looked at it and said that it was interesting but there weren't enough wide shots in it. I was so shaken because I didn't know what he was talking about – wide shots, what were they? After that I became obsessed by studying shots and working out what the guy was talking about. There is an important grammar there which can influence the feel and look of a film. I was really interested in that at film school. Some of my films were quite stiff because I was so obsessed with shots. But then I had my eyes open about what you can do. Form and content have to have a good, easy relationship with each other. A lot of people achieve that relationship pretty fast; I'm quite slow and look at every way you can shoot a scene. I always turn up with the shot list.

I come from art school so I like to think and draw at the same time. I like to think about the theme through drawing, not to say everything won't change dramatically, but I find it helps a lot, and I start to think of the way it looks. At first I like the film to tell me what it needs to be by itself and then I identify ten or 20 scenes which are pivotal and work out the style in those. I start to think whether they will look good in shadow or light and work out the mood and coverage. I do all this storyboarding myself. I make sure I write down what these key scenes are. I describe them to myself and what I want to achieve in them. I might base all my thinking around five scenes. In **Holy Smoke**, for example, a crucial scene is the one where the family surrounds Ruth and she realises there's been a big deception. You know that you're going to change the tone and mood of the movie in that scene, and I had to try and make that transition smoothly and truthfully. Another one is when she is naked and wets herself, and you don't know whether she is lost to herself or if it's a trick. Another is when she and Harvey Keitel make love for the first time. And so on.

Sometimes you want to lock the blocking down because a scene is going to be complicated and will be shot over a few days, but in general I don't like to have too many prerequisites about what the actors should do, in order that they can find the scene truthfully themselves. I'll work out how to film it after I've been through it with the actors, and that's where you have to get clever and think on your feet. It's not your shots that are going to count, it's just getting out of their way and having their work on screen that counts.

The writing is just a stage for me. When I begin directing I don't care very much for the writing. The actors are more loyal to it than I am. I believe it doesn't really matter because it's not what you're going to be seeing on the screen. It's a guide, but once we get on set, I want everybody to just let the script go and explore because now we're doing the real thing. We spend more time working it out on set than I did when I was writing it. Quite often, I have had to argue with my cast over my own writing.

I've got the film in my head. I'm doing the checks and balances all the time. Going into the film is the most mentally weighty time in my life because I've written the film, been preparing it for four months, been rehearsing for three or four weeks, and you've got the entire film in your head. You've got maybe 400 or 500 shots in your head, then every day for the next 15 weeks, you start shedding ten of them here, 15 of them here, and it just feels great, lighter and lighter as it goes along. You may find that on the first day of rehearsal, which was a month before you started shooting, you discovered stuff which you have to remember 15 weeks into the shoot. In other words, you have to remember all these details 19 weeks later, so you have to be really responsible and keep notes. It's a lot of homework. It's never been possible for me to shoot in sequence. I've never had the budget or the personality to command that kind of control. Because you've rehearsed it so extensively, the actors have it in their head. I try and shoot a hallmark scene early on to see in the rushes if there's the right feel to the work, or the right look.

I relate to the actors probably because my mother's an actress and my father's a theatre director, so I've heard talk about acting all my life. But when it comes to the actors, more than any other thing, I think I have a good friendship with them. I love them and I'm really interested in their problems. When I was making the short films, I started to think about how to communicate with actors so that they had enough freedom, while at the same time giving myself what I wanted. On **Sweetie** and the early films, I was a bit of a dictator, but loveable and kind enough to them that it wasn't a problem.

Actors are my voice and I will give them whatever I can of me, but I know that they have to reach the high notes by themselves. I can stop an actor falling over but I can't reach their spectacular moments. That's only something I can be there to witness, but it's quite phenomenal to be on the set when an actor is doing something extraordinary, and nobody else on the set knows it. They've struck gold and no-one's seen it. And that happens so many times.

I think it's exciting for men and women working together on one of my movies as it's a different sort of dynamic with me; certainly for Harvey Keitel and even Sam Neill on **The Piano**, we have a different quality to our relationship than men would have with a male director. It's softer and sexier and more honest. The deal is that we tell the truth as we know it or as far as we can find it, and that's always very exciting. And when you're working with people who aren't frightened of that, there's nothing as exciting.

I know that some scenes are going to be visual statements, so I just work them out visually, and during rehearsals I will say to the actors, "hey guys, please be puppets on this occasion because that scene will not be about your character, it just sets up the atmosphere or the character of the movie". On the other hand, there will be scenes about two actors responding, in which case it's up to me to follow the actors and find a way to make the camera show what they're doing. Sometimes the camera leads and sometimes the drama leads.

1

2

3

(1–4) **The Portrait of a Lady**: (1) Storyboard from the travelogue scene in the film, which Campion points to as one of her favourites. Prior to a year-long trip with Madame Merle (Barbara Hershey), Isabel Archer (Nicole Kidman) meets Gilbert Osmond (John Malkovich) and falls in love with him. "We wanted to go to the Pyramids originally but didn't have the budget, so I worked out the travelogue. She's become really obsessed, and there's a nice little moment where I had to illustrate this. I put the couple into old newsreel footage on a blue screen. It was a playful version of the trip. All Isabel could do was think of the person she's left behind. Isn't that typical that you meet someone significant just before an overseas trip?"

4

1

3

2

4

(1–2) Making **Sweetie**, for just A$900,000, was an eye-opening experience for Campion, who says that she was "so naive. I thought my job as a director was to be the hostess, and I wanted everything to be nice and wanted to be liked by everybody. Creatively, however, I was as stubborn and strong as you could hope." **Sweetie** was a "full-blown realisation" of the work she had done at film school, a film notable for the striking visual style she conceived with her cinematographer Sally Bongers. "Sally and I played with the frame and had no sense of being daring, because that was just how we were expressing ourselves. When our producer saw the rushes, he started panting with excitement, but we had storyboarded it all and didn't think anything of it." (3–4) **An Angel at My Table** told the story, in three 52-minute TV episodes (and one 156-minute feature), of writer Janet Frame, and how eight years in shock therapy in a mental institution almost ruins her life. Campion is characteristically self-critical about the films. "I liked the first episode which is a really very honest, sweet tale of childhood but the rest feels like TV and I don't like it."

84

directing

I'm more interested now in what humans are able to communicate together or how they can be together. That's less limiting than when someone was only allowed to stand in one corner of the frame.

I hate sentiment, which I believe is a distortion of truth. Truth is the only way into the centre of the whole mystery of life, and if you start to distort or discredit or confuse it, that's a big treachery. Lack of sentiment informs my whole life. If I realise something is true, I have to move in that direction, no matter how inconvenient or how difficult it is. Emotion and sentimentality are entirely different and have got nothing to do with each other. Sentimentality is a manipulation of feeling for a result, where emotionality is an honest result of something in the story, without an intended manipulation.

Most of my films are written about women, and people often ask why I make films about women. It's like someone saying, "why do you speak English?" It's as basic as that to me. I think the reason that actresses have excelled in my films is that I'm speaking in their language; I'm speaking through the body of a woman, the psyche of a woman, and that's my particular insight.

I honestly think that there are so many more people that have as much if not a lot more talent than me, but what I don't know is fear. I don't get paranoid. I get so excited by the idea of what fun it will be to do something that I can't see any fear. That is a huge, huge freedom. I see people paralysed by fear all the time, and of course, in other areas of my life I'm paralysed by it, but not creatively. Later, when I show the film, then I start getting nervous, but I am having too much fun when I'm making a movie. It's play for me.

Campion talks fondly of her leading ladies — all of whom have given exceptional performances in her films. "It's a great privilege to work with these forces of nature." (above) Campion with Kate Winslet on the set of **Holy Smoke**.

biography

Born in Taiwan in 1954, Ang Lee moved to the US in 1978 and graduated with his MFA from New York University Film School. After two award-winning shorts, he raised $400,000 to direct **Pushing Hands (Tui Shou**, 1991), his feature-film debut about a Chinese American who brings his tai-chi master father to live with him in New York. **Pushing Hands** marked the start of his working relationship with James

ang lee

Schamus (writer and co-producer) and Ted Hope (producer). Lee's second film **The Wedding Banquet (Xiyan**, 1993), began his writing collaboration with Schamus, and again examined cultural differences between Taiwanese and Americans in New York; it won him the Golden Bear for Best Film at the Berlin Film Festival. His third, **Eat Drink Man Woman (Yin She Nan Nu**, 1994), shot in Taiwan, was even more successful, winning Lee an international following and a directing job on Columbia Pictures' 1995 adaptation of Jane Austen's 'Sense and Sensibility'. While this well-loved film was chiefly perceived as a triumph for actress and screenwriter Emma Thompson, Lee's skilful direction is at the heart of its success. He followed it with the acclaimed **The Ice Storm** (1997) and a $35 million American Civil War epic **Ride with the Devil** in 1999. But it was **Crouching Tiger, Hidden Dragon (Wo Hu Cang Long**, 2000), which won him his biggest following. Shot entirely in China and in Mandarin, it is the biggest grossing non-English-language film in history and won Lee virtually every award going. He is currently working on a version of Marvel Comics' 'The Hulk'.

interview

I grew up with Hollywood movies and Chinese mainstream movies. The first thing I watched with artistic mentality was **The Graduate**, which was five years old by the time it came to Taiwan. That was during my first year out of high school, 1973, and that was the first time I was aware of something which was not just storytelling. A year later I saw **The Virgin Spring** by Ingmar Bergman which was truly inspiring, then **Bicycle Thieves** and films by Antonioni and Kurosawa. Neo-realism in Italian film is something I could never get away from. Those films transcended that very earthly tone to something on a higher level, philosophically and socialistically. So before I learned how to resist the influence of other film-makers, they were the ones that influenced me.

At that stage I wasn't admitting I was a film-maker. I was still ashamed. Years after graduating from film school, before I made my first movie, I still couldn't admit that I was a film-maker. After I came to the US, I got the chance to watch a lot more art films, and there was a time when I was rebellious towards the culture I came from, because I realised the

Eastern way of life is very anti-drama in a way to make you more docile. In the West, it's about a world upside down, it's about exhilaration, the ultimate personality. All the sexual and dramatic influences emphasised in Western culture have been my main influence. So during that period, I was attracted to films with a rebellious nature, like Buñuel's.

In New York I was developing one thing after another. Nothing was getting made, it was hell. You just keep rewriting and rewriting. It takes a year or two years, and you live in hope. But through this process, I began to learn how a feature-length script functions through the baffling experience of rewrites, and also how a mainstream film requires a film-maker to be. It's a good experience, allowing you to discover what the requirements of the mainstream are and whether you fit into them.

The usual form of movies is about two hours – at least 90 minutes. After I made short films at school, it took me years to figure out two things – first, that a movie is different from drama, it's more stretched out, and second, the function in the character development and the structure is not necessarily the storytelling. So you may have lots of ideas that may be good ideas, but they may not hold your attention for two hours. What appeals to me is usually the philosophic thought of what type of movie I can make. For example, with **The Ice Storm**, I got to do something cubic rather than what I was already familiar with, which was narrative film-making, which is linear in structure. In **The Ice Storm** I knew that I wanted to hit that emotional core, maybe through different routes, but eventually I would arrive at that core. I would backtrack to how I would need to start it in order to drive it to that point, usually towards the end, so it's like I can count backwards to

decide how to start it and how to develop it. That excites me. It's an emotional hit, probably at the final moment or through a structure that I thought would be very interesting enough for people to glue their eyes onto the screen for at least 90 minutes or two hours. Or a subject matter that I think is important to me at that point in my life. Usually the projects have a very philosophical side to them, and then I have to reduce that in the movie-making process because you don't want to really show it, it's just the thought actually before the emotion that will hit me first, get me excited. Then there's the story part: you make up a story – that's your job, that's the least you can do.

In the most part, the scripts I receive are by professional writers working within the Hollywood system. The scripts have had a group effort put into them and they are built like battleships. There is no way you could make a mistake directing them. In fact, anyone could direct them. You don't get to do the film-maker thing. My close friend and collaborator James Schamus doesn't over-write. He doesn't need to prove in the script that the movie will be unsinkable. He lets me do my film.

I can do a genre piece like **Crouching Tiger, Hidden Dragon** and there are certain obligations concerning how to deliver it – i.e. you have to have 30 minutes of fight sequences – but I would want to have some kind of twist. I like mixing the genres. It's more fun. For example on **The Ice Storm**, I used techniques from **Invasion of the Bodysnatchers** for the storm itself, so I fused the techniques of a disaster movie into a family drama. I got a kick out of that because the film was set in 1973 and disaster movies were the most popular movie genre in that year. The ice creeps up and

1

2

3

4

5

6

7

8

9

10

(1–10) **Crouching Tiger, Hidden Dragon** saw Ang Lee shoot in Hong Kong and China in a genre which is a staple of Hong Kong cinema. (8) "The first fight in **Crouching Tiger** was so time consuming because me and the choreographer were standing imagining how to do the movement on the spot while everybody was waiting. I would lay out the set, the theme, and the principle of how that works for the chasing sequence. In the film, Michelle Yeoh [Shu Lien] is a grounded woman so she doesn't know the flying technique, but she's so quick and experienced she can still catch the flying leader at a slow pace. So that's the principle – one quick, one slow. One graceful, one almost running. So you've got to have a story or it's just bang, bang, bang. The theme of the combat is that she doesn't let her fly away. Whenever she tries to fly out, she grabs her to nail her. That was the whole point of the story originally: that Shu Lien is trying to ground Jen [Zhang Ziyi] but she keeps flying. Eventually Shu Lien loses all she loves, but that doesn't stop Jen from flying away."

1

2

3

4

(1–4) **Crouching Tiger, Hidden Dragon**: "My cinematographer was Peter Pau, who is the biggest cameraman in Hong Kong. I think his aesthetic sense and experience in working on martial arts films and American movies were right for this film. He had experience coping with people like fight choreographer Yuen Wo Ping, who is a special type of Hong-Kong film-maker full of raw energy, but also he can handle spontaneous film-making shot in sequence and still make it look good. He used the power-pod camera which I had used to little effect in the US, but these guys in Hong Kong, they use it like hand-held... The flying scenes have become more affordable because you can remove the wires digitally, but they are still a combination of the craftsmanship in Hong Kong, the wire work, the hands, the craft that coordinate between action and skill. It's real skill, without machines, which culminated in the forest scene (2, 4), which was the most difficult scene because you have no ground, so you had to mimic something soft and swaying."

it's deep, it cuts across everything and freezes everything together and in a way it's horrifying. The very idea of the ice storm was enough for me to take up the challenge.

I don't like storyboarding. I did it on my first two student films, and I spent a lot of time drawing. I still do it to help the visualising and communicating between me and the crew, and they are often more secure when they see something in drawing, but it's silly to make a motion picture through a series of still pictures. It has to be moving. There's something intangible about it. To me the film-making process doesn't end until the last note you put on the final mix, and until that time, you are still in search of the movie. I would refuse to do a movie to fit the picture. I trust my instinct, my movie sense, my own vision and see what happens spontaneously, because you're watching the real thing instead of a still picture somebody's drawing.

When I'm working on a script with James Schamus, I always force him to come up with one word to sum up the essence of a scene or a movie – to sum up the core emotional feeling or the taste of the movie. For **The Ice Storm**, it was "embarrassment". The way I rehearsed with Kevin Kline was to try to destroy his confidence, because that's what his character is about. He doesn't know what he's doing, he's utterly uncomfortable. He doesn't know how to be open with his kids, he doesn't have the skill to educate them or be their role model. So by the time the key party comes along, embarrassment is the real essence, and then "edge". I talked to the cameraman about portraying "edge", like ice breaking. I would rather use something abstract like a word or two than use a storyboard.

We spend two to three weeks before principal photography in rehearsal. It varies from movie to movie, because sometimes we need to do training, like on **Sense and Sensibility** the actors needed to learn how to walk, dance, hold themselves, or on **Ride with the Devil** ride horses, shoot a gun or boot camp. I initiate those classes and participate in them. Some, like **The Ice Storm**, are simple rehearsals, but they are important as a time for the actors to get the essence of the part they're playing. It's not like theatre rehearsing, where you refine everything. In a film, you shoot moment by moment and you don't want to over-rehearse them like a basketball-team coach. You don't want to use up the best energy practising for the game. They have to look their best and be most spontaneous and fresh for take after take out of sequence, so rehearsing is a way of getting a taste for the characters. That's the process when I know my actors and when they decide that you are the director.

Then of course there's the rehearsal on shooting days, where we will block early in the morning. Blocking is one of the most important crafts in direction, I think. You have to quickly block it spontaneously because actors might not go where you want them to. That's the biggest training I got from **Sense and Sensibility**, where I had fewer oratory skills or knowledge about blocking in general, how to restrict their movements or how to be sensitive to what they like to do and why they would want to do something. Actors put their images in your hands, they trust you, so you have to be trustworthy, and that takes time. Image wasn't something very strong in my head. Now I know how to cope with it better and I can make quick decisions. You have to establish your authority not only with the actors but with the crew members. 50 people are watching you, and if the actors don't look like they're comfortable or know what they're doing, that could be the beginning of the collapse of discipline. **Sense and Sensibility** was great training for me. I wasn't in the major league yet, and after that film, I was established. When I got onto **The Ice Storm**, I was more established, and also American actors are more comfortable with the camera. You can put a camera on the back of their head and they won't turn around, whereas English actors have a way of working their way towards the camera.

Sometimes I have to avoid the actor altogether and make the movie in a more Chinese way. In **Sense and Sensibility**, which was the first time I used this method, the landscape, the colour and the lines gave guidance to where the emotion went. I think by visualising a theme, that theme reflects a mentality and reflects moods when you're watching it. So when you echo your character in the visual picture, I think that's very cinematically useful. It has been applied in all kinds of Chinese art forms, whether in poetry or painting – they always start off from the picture. So when you see Marianne [Kate Winslet], this incredibly romantic character, drawing the surrounding landscape against a backdrop of that same landscape, and artificially bringing it to life, that was the theme of the time. I wanted to see those landscapes. What does grey mean? What does blue mean? What visually gives guidance? If you put clouds there or exaggerate the greenness, that implies craziness and that has to do with the craziness of passion, whereas the strict lines of hedges give the sense of sense.

I will treasure the moment when Marianne goes crazy and goes up to the hedge and recites a Shakespeare sonnet in a storm, because it's a film-maker's moment. I would also do

things like put Emma Thompson in a navy blue gown and in a square door frame, and contrast her with her mother going crazy. It helps the drama. In a tacit way, this has a great impact on the audience. Like in **Eat Drink Man Woman**, the table is full of beautiful-looking dishes but your mouth only waters because you've just seen how it was cooked step-by-step. And then you have to make the audience hungry by having actors talk over the table without touching the food – it's just torture. That's implicit film-making. That adds up. And then they put it away in the refrigerator, and everybody stays thin. Nobody touches the food, they just look at it and talk about their life and their problems, or they miscommunicate. Implicitly, the food is hypnotising, and somehow at the end when she has a taste again and she serves him some soup, you are moved. You don't know why, but it's movie magic.

I think those are very important elements in the craft of making movies. It's the unseen, the untold – like putting a frame behind Emma when she's just watching, you can still do your lines, she can still do her acting whatever, you can still show good footage to the studio. But you sneak that in. Yeah. I think the person who did that best was Hitchcock, and the more I grow up the more I admire him. That sneaky bastard – that's great craftsmanship.

I think making movies is only half, the first half of the film process. The second half is film appreciation, it's the audience, both the paying audience and critics alike. I refuse to think, even though, like every film-maker, I hate critics sometimes, that just because they never made a movie they don't have a right to analyse them. That counts too. So the audience counts, although you don't have to do things to

(1–4) **The Ice Storm**: Working with a sterling ensemble of US actors, Lee created an emotionally devastating portrait of dysfunctional family life and human miscommunication in **The Ice Storm**, adapted from the novel by Rick Moody. He looks back with awe at his experiences of working with actors on such sensitive material. "One of my favourite scenes is Kevin Kline looking through reflective glass in his underwear by a cloud of swinging olive trees. He's almost naked in his socks and he looks lost. Another favourite is when Joan Allen comes back to the bathroom and talks to Kevin after she has had casual sex with a neighbour in the car. All I had to say to her was, 'do you still love this guy?', and she just burst into tears and couldn't stop. It was the last shot of the day, and we did 13 takes over one hour. I had to give directions, not only emotional but technical, so there were numerous marks she had to take so as not to block Kevin, but she was sobbing and shaking the whole time. She didn't cry during the scene, she just had to tremble. That was a pretty intense experience for me." (4) The ice storm hits.

1

Many eyebrows were raised when Lee went from his Chinese ensemble **Eat Drink Man Woman** (1) to the big league Hollywood adaptation of **Sense and Sensibility** (2–3), although he identifies common themes in all his work. "The films are all about compromise – when the characters have to compromise and accept certain facts, and when they have to accept the fact of changing. When I did **Sense and Sensibility**, I found that part of the essence of the subtext of life was really about the conflict between sense and sensibility, and I express that in the film through the tension between personal free will and social obligations. The enigmatic nature of conflict, like the yin and the yang, is something that I always portray. It's like breathing; I couldn't get away with it not being the essence of each movie." **Sense and Sensibility** was such a challenge for Lee that he applied a Chinese regard to the landscapes (3) (discussed on page 92). (right) Lee on the set of **Ride with the Devil**.

2

3

please your audience, but you have to put that in your consciousness, because it's an activity of communication. Film is not a diary, it's expression, and there has to be reception, so I have various audiences in mind for different things I do in a film.

I don't think film-making craft passes from one person to another. I love Bergman and would love to do something equivalent to him, but it would turn out too me, and I cannot duplicate his craft. He's a different person. You have to find your own way in how your personality applies to time, craft, equipment, money, cast and crew, light or even location. It's not just making the movie, it's how you deal with life. I look like a nice person and I appear to be trustworthy. I use certain techniques to lure the best out of an actor or get a cinematographer to do the things I want him to do. If I was too tough, I don't think it would work. It's just the way I make movies. I work very closely with everyone. Every sound you hear, every line, every little breath, I make them together with my team. I work with the effects people, not to mention the editor and every cutter.

What's the same in all my movies is my personality. If I do a brutal scene, people will be shocked watching it. If Quentin Tarantino did a brutal scene, people might laugh and oddly enjoy it. People perceive it differently because you are different personalities. On each film you make hundreds of decisions daily, every one a struggle and every one done as the best thing for the moment, but when you put it all together, it still comes out as a reflection of your personality.

biography

Taught by Martin Scorsese, among others, at New York University Film School in the class of 1971, Oliver Stone ultimately joined Scorsese in the sparsely populated ranks of American cinema visionaries. Relentlessly energetic, angry, violent, sometimes overpowering, often didactic and always visually inspired, Stone's canon of in-your-face slices of Americana is one of the defining bodies of work of the end-of-

oliver stone

century cinema. Squarely tackling varied subjects, Stone makes big, bold movies designed for mass audiences with a high rate of hits. Stone first achieved fame as a writer, winning an Oscar for **Midnight Express** in 1978. It wasn't until 1986, when he wrote and directed both **Salvador** and **Platoon** (the latter loosely based on his own experiences on tours of duties in the Vietnam War), that he achieved renown as a director. One of the great war films of all time, **Platoon** kicked off another two Vietnam-themed pictures: **Born on the Fourth of July** (1989) and **Heaven & Earth** (1993), but it was **JFK** in 1991 which elevated Stone to new levels of infamy and influence. Dramatising the assassination of John F. Kennedy and the conspiracies that could have caused it, **JFK** sealed Stone's reputation as an opinion-divider and controversy-magnet, tags which he has hardly worked to lose with subsequent films, notably the violent road movie **Natural Born Killers** (1994) and biopic **Nixon** (1995). Stone's other films include **Wall Street** (1987), **The Doors** (1991), **U Turn** (1997) and **Any Given Sunday** (1999).

interview

I'm a writer and director and co-producer – in other words you could say film-maker. Writing is the dirtiest job; you're spending six to eight hours a day alone. There's nothing quite like that feeling of loneliness, doubt and an ultimate trust in your personal view of the world.

Directing is the focal point of the process for me. It begins with writing, goes through directing and editing and, unfortunately, the modern world has added this fourth phase called marketing and release, which has become a nightmare unto itself. Often by the time the director finishes a film, he'll feel like a trash barrel in hell, and it's then that he has to represent himself and his film to the world. Then somebody comes along and just breaks his heart with some two-hour verdict based often on a mindset or a snap pre-judgement. But it takes some looking. The films to me represent a huge outburst of energy and detail, and when I'm often criticised for being direct or heavy-handed, it always amazes me that those people are not at least noting the "levels" of different actions going on simultaneously on the screen. I think I make dimensional three-ring circuses, or try to. And because it's busy doesn't mean it's shallow or it has attention-deficit disorder; on the contrary, it requires more attention. So I guess for me, as with many other directors, it's a masochistic process. It's harder and harder without critical respect. You must from the get-go believe in the sound of one hand clapping. That's the only thing you'll get out of this thing.

I've tried not to make the same film twice. I reach a place in my life, I intersect the movie at a certain space and time, and that's when I say goodbye or modify the old self because it's no longer working as well. When I write myself, I basically make the scenes believable to myself as a director so that I can dramatise them. If I read somebody else's script, and I cannot understand how or why I should do this scene, then I have to rewrite it, and if they don't want me to rewrite it, I have to find another script. Credibility is the issue. On a recent movie, we went through eight drafts with a very good writer but, while it had very good things in it, it wasn't working as a whole. It's crucial for a director to understand that the whole is more important than the parts. I've done movies where I've worked so hard on the parts that I lost sight of the whole, and often you suffer in the editing room, which is the reverse of writing. Writing is the key to the movie, the way in; editing the way out. I have done so much readjusting of the script in editing rooms, there's been so much creativity and moving things around. If you look at the original scripts and see what we did with the structure, you'll see that everything is fluid. It's up for grabs in rehearsal, in directing, again in the editing, but writing itself is the beginning, the core, the beginning of the description we bring to our lives. Some people think I'm primarily a writer, and I use the camera like a big typewriter trying to make the point. Far

from it – I feel that the directing is a process and it grows with the actors and the cinematographer and the designers because they collaborate, and it becomes such a thing unto itself that it grows into another beast.

When I'm writing, I become very internalised. But directing is a more social, people-oriented skill and I think myself good at bringing people out of themselves into new possibilities. Yes, you're the prime visionary but you're also the guider, you have to be Tiresias in the underworld, taking people to a place that they've often never been before and of which they have apprehensions. So do I, of course. I don't know whether I will come out at the other end, but I think there's a light at the end of the tunnel. You take these people down into Hades and then all together you seek the light.

Every film has its own series of pitfalls, quagmires and sand traps, and you have to be very flexible. Rigidity doesn't work for me. I always felt that good directors are like bamboo, they're strong but they yield. The director has to have an ego to survive, but at the same time his ego must not get in the way of letting the actors and other key players emerge and flower. It's his job in a sense to sublimate himself and let them rise so that the whole idea of the tyrannical director is a contradiction in terms. It makes no sense: no good director can be a tyrant and succeed because he would not be allowing his actors the freedom they need to explore their characters.

Rehearsal is an important demarcation for many directors, and I know some who think that if they've done rehearsal before they go to the set, it's ready. That's probably a more disciplined method from the studio days. I always look at rehearsal as a pre-event. If you can do it two or three times

1

2

3

4

(1–5) **Natural Born Killers**: Stone was one of the first film-makers to use Lightworks and Avid editing machines on **The Doors** in 1991, machines which give him, he says, "tremendous freedom". Of **Natural Born Killers**, Stone says, "It was the first film where I boldly cut to my own mind face. I tried it a little on **JFK**, but because **Natural Born** was fiction, I could do what I wanted more. You can see Tom Sizemore and Tommy Lee Jones (1) walking down the prison hall. It's an insane walk, and the cutaways are insane and with the rhythm and the timing, they go through several musical variations as they go through several halls. The scene works because at one point we cut to a butterfly, at which point the music and the butterfly blend. We wanted an image of beauty at this point juxtaposed with the ugliness." The whole shoot was "pretty wild", if only because he shot scenes with rear projectors on set (4). "We went over budget on that film because rear projection is still very unwieldy and we were actually hauling this huge projector around Arizona, New Mexico and Chicago."

5

1

directing

2

3

(1–3) Stone took Quentin Tarantino's original screenplay for **Natural Born Killers** and adapted it to his own style. "I would never take a Tarantino approach to violence, and I think you can see the difference in **Natural Born**. In **Pulp Fiction**, he looks at violence with irony and thinks it's funny, and I could never do that because I've been in a war. It's just different approaches. I took his script and overhauled it, but we used the basis of a very brilliant idea and went much further into society as it existed in the '90s in America. I was shocked that the film was so misunderstood. I mean, how can you take a satire like that so seriously?"

4

5

6

(4–6) Working with a mammoth cast of both real athletes and actors on **Any Given Sunday** was, "very hard because they were all demanding attention. Football players usually only play for a few hours at a time and I was asking for 12 hours a day, so there were so many demands on me and I found it physically exhausting. I've reached a place where I've done 14 movies as a director, seven as a writer, 12 as a producer, and I would now like to make movies on my terms rather than be miserable again. Movies are painful and you can't run from pain. You have to go out and hustle, but at the same time you have to keep the dream together."

before shooting with some success, that's a way of getting examples to bounce off in your thinking or feeling, but ultimately it comes down to the day you shoot. You end up doing some version which combines elements of the three or four things you did in rehearsal from different reads or interpretations. I insist on rehearsal – a two-week rehearsal around the last three weeks on location or in a master place where all the actors come. It's a very intense process, and then I rewrite the last week before shooting because that's my last chance, although I'm also doing a dozen other things.

In rehearsal you have to listen to some of the ideas, and maintain your judgement so that you can correct the script in constructive ways. Writing is the most time-consuming thing. That's why they say that if you have to rewrite on set, you get killed financially. I've been in that position where I've had to rewrite at night and you're trying to fix something and it's really ridiculous and wasteful because it's costing $150,000 a day to shoot. Talk about paralysis. Who wants to be under that kind of pressure? When I visited Fellini on the set of **La Voce della Luna** in Rome, I went to see him at around 11 o' clock in the morning and he was having problems in a scene with Roberto Benigni. And at lunch, he rewrote the scene and came back that afternoon and they filmed it in the afternoon. I wouldn't want to be in that position. If an actor says we can say something a shorter way, I often embrace it because, as a director, you're always trying to take four sentences and make them three. You're often trying to find the cleanest, simplest way to say something, unless it's a character's idiosyncrasy.

Many directors will tell you that the five to eight weeks before a movie actually shoots are the worst, because you're preparing, sometimes over-preparing, and because nothing has yet been achieved, you feel as if you're wandering in a mist. I've seen some good films which I know weren't prepped very well and I know some directors who are very talented who don't rehearse at all, but I don't know how they do it.

Part of me is still at New York University Film School, where 35mm was a luxury and we had to struggle to get four minutes of black and white, so to get 65 days to shoot a movie is really a privilege. I've kept to 50 to 68 days on all my shoots except **JFK** (72 days), unlike some indulgent directors who I think are ruining the business by shooting small domestic dramas in 80 to 100 day spans. I would much rather lose $3 million, which we did on **Noriega**, preparing a very complicated movie with many scripts, than make it and lose a financier $40 to 50 million. Al Pacino and I read **Noriega** twice over a month-and-a-half period with two different groups of actors, and it just didn't work the first time, and it was worse the second. We looked at each other and knew it was pointless to make this movie because it did not have anything close to an integrity of tone. In fact, it would've been a disaster. It was the best decision we could've made. Not to do it.

The actors and I have usually had great relationships. I've tried to make them work in a direction that's fresh to me. Nobody really thought Anthony Hopkins could do **Nixon**, or Michael Douglas **Wall Street**, or Tom Cruise **Born on the Fourth of July**. Woody Harrelson had never done a movie like **Natural Born Killers** before, but I strongly felt a fun and madness in him that was perfect for Mickey; Juliette Lewis as well had been a sweet girl in **Cape Fear**, yet she blended savagely and authentically into Mallory. I will never forget her in that performance, or Woody, Tom [Sizemore],

(1–12) Stone points to **Nixon** as one of his towering achievements. "I think **Nixon** is one of the biggest challenges I ever had. **JFK** had a lot of thunder and lightning and it's probably the most ambitious film I tried, and I'm probably the proudest of that because I went for the biggest I could, but **Nixon** is really complex and it had very little props. I had white men in pretty ugly suits talking for most of the movie. It's not really a movie of sex or violence, there's nothing in there, Richard Nixon's an unsexy fellow and yet personally I find it so intricate, between the dialogue and the flashbacks, that it generates a lot of tension. That's what I'm very proud of, that I've created tension from pure dialogue." (5–10) Extracts from shooting scripts for **Nixon** with Stone's comments.

(Revised Blue Page May 5, 1995)   69.

                    HAROLD (panting)
        Hey... you'll be able to do it now.

                    RICHARD
        Do what...?

                    HAROLD
        Go to law school. Mom and Dad'll be able to afford
        it now...

        Richard looks at him in horror.

                    HAROLD
        Mom expects great things from you...

                    RICHARD
        Harold... can I get you anything?

        Harold throws a loving arm around Richard, who tenses. We
        sense Harold in some way could have helped Richard, taught
        him to laugh a bit.

                    HAROLD (a gentle smile)
        Relax, Dick, it's just me... The desert's so
        beautiful, isn't it? (then) I want to go home,
        Dick, time to go home.

                    RICHARD (stiffly)
        You're not gonna quit on me, are you, Harold?

        Harold looks out over the landscape. Silence.

        56 INT. NIXON HOUSE - PARLOR - NIGHT (1933)   56

        RICHARD sits staring into the fire. He still wears his black
        suit from Harold's funeral. HANNAH enters quietly.

                    HANNAH
        Richard?

        He looks up at her.

                    RICHARD
        I can't...

                    HANNAH
        Thee must.

        She moves closer. Casting a shadow over his face.

                    HANNAH
        It's a gift, Richard. This law school is a gift
        from your brother.

(Revised Yellow Page May 30, 1995)   70.

                    RICHARD (bitter)
        Did he have to die for me to get it!

                    HANNAH
        It's meant to make us stronger. (kneels) Thee
        art stronger than Harold... stronger than Arthur.
        God has chosen thee to survive...

                    RICHARD
        What about happiness, Mother?

                    HANNAH
        Thee must find thy peace at the center, Richard.
        Strength in this life. Happiness in the next.

                                            DISSOLVE TO:

        57 INT. REPUBLICAN CONVENTION - NIGHT (1968)   57

        ON RICHARD NIXON (55) -- in his prime. A profile of his face
        -- as the vast crowd goes beserk. Nixon absorbs the
        adoration -- at last, he has arrived. He looks down at
        someone in the audience. Points, smiles, waves.

        Then he steps forward, thrusts his arms in the air -- the
        twin V salute. The cheers rattle the hall as PAT and his
        DAUGHTERS join him, followed by Vice-President SPIRO AGNEW
        and his FAMILY. Nixon puts his arm around Pat. She waves.
        The crowd is on its feet.

                    NIXON (privately to Pat)
        Now tell me you didn't want this, Buddy.

        Pat smiles back at him, caught up in it. Then she kisses him
        on the cheek.

                                            TIME CUT TO:

        NIXON addresses the DELEGATES.

                    NIXON
        America is in trouble today not because her people
        have failed but because her leaders have failed.
        When the strongest nation in the world can be tied
        down for four years in a war in Vietnam with no
        end in sight; when the richest nation in the world
        can't manage its own economy; when the nation with
        the greatest tradition of the rule of law is
        plagued by unprecedented lawlessness; when a
        nation that has been known for a century for
        equality of opportunity is torn by unprecedented
        racial violence; and when the President of the
        United States cannot travel abroad or to any major
        city at home without fear of a hostile

8   9   10

Nixon: Stone cites Anthony Hopkins and Al Pacino as two of the most masterful and "delightful" actors he has worked with. "The director/actor relationship has to be honest to explore acting, and there was no ego with Tony and Al in the sense that we had really honest relationships. I try to make very concrete, specific suggestions after every take – I don't come up with something abstract. With Tony, for example, I must have made a thousand suggestions and he's like an instrument you can play because he tried every single one of them. Al was the same. He was able to take criticism and, even though he didn't agree sometimes, he would try out my suggestions." (11) Stone with Anthony Hopkins who played Richard Nixon.

11

12

Tommy Lee [Jones], and Robert Downey Jr. I'm not always saying counter-cast. You can't cast somebody who's not strong and expect them to be strong. They have to have some strength, or basis of the quality required, to begin with.

I work with multiple editors because one editor is too slow a process for me. I like to be the supervising editor bringing together different styles and points of view. I liked it in my New York University Film School days, when we would sit around and collectively criticise other people's films, and I try and recreate that in the editing suite. On **Any Given Sunday**, I had five editors. As a result, a critic wrote that it was "corporate art", but it wasn't at all because I had a strong vision over it all. Nothing goes out, not one frame, without my approval. The editors work in several different rooms and we come together a few times a week to show what they've done to the group, so we get a group reaction. We become very tight in this way. Alongside this, the process of screening outside the group goes on. You show it to people you trust and work on getting it to expand.

Sometimes you fool yourself. What could be great on the day in the editing process doesn't work out. Conversely, some stuff that you may think is not great does turn out to be much better because there is something hidden there. I don't think any director can always get it right. Those '40s directors were so confident, but it's a different world now with more ambiguity in our behaviour. Billy Wilder, yes, could cut a film in 11 or 12 days because he knew what he wanted. Hitchcock was the same.

Any Given Sunday, we jumped around between eight and ten characters. You can make a more powerful movie if you stay with one person, like on Denzel Washington in **The Hurricane**, but I wanted to jump around, tell a story through a tableaux of people like **Grand Hotel**. We live very monochromatically in the sense that we allow terms to be dictated to us. A film has to be neo-realist or post-modern. That is so boring. Let's be like painters and have six or ten different styles existing at the same time. We could try cubistic film-making at the same time as other people are doing naturalistic film-making or super-realistic or post-modern film-making.

Critics tend to personalise films, but ultimately the writer-director is an illusion. He's presenting a journey through which he went, but it doesn't mean he is that character. I've been criticised often for being a Vietnam veteran, for hating women, for being humourless. One film I'm a drugged-out Jim Morrison, the next a paranoid Richard Nixon, or a square Jim Garrison. How can I be all those people? The real me is in parts not at all easy to figure out.

At the moment, I'm writing a story about a woman [**Beyond Borders**, a project which he has since abandoned] and I'm trying to throw myself into her. You could call it a gender transfer. It doesn't mean I am that character. The truth of the matter is that most people don't think about you for more than ten seconds in their life, and when they do it's with some glib cartoon or caricature. With me, it's Vietnam or a conspiracy theorist, even though I've also made a *film noir*, a football movie, a film about a paranoid president and **Natural Born Killers**. But it's the nature of American culture to be glib and one-dimensional. I just got to keep going my way. Sometimes every time I'm on TV I think I'm another person depending which year it is, which film – which ring of the tree really.

4

5

oliver stone

6

7

(1–7) **U Turn** was Stone's 1997 attempt at *film noir*. It starred an impressive cast led by Sean Penn, Nick Nolte, Jennifer Lopez, Joaquin Phoenix and Billy Bob Thornton. "It's a very sick movie, but I loved it because again it's misunderstood. To me it was truly *noir*. In the new *noir*, there are happy endings but in the old *noir* everybody dies. And **U Turn** adheres rigidly to that formula, because everybody dies out of their greed or stupidity or wrong choices. I called it *film soleil* at the time because it was shot in the sunshine. And I got *spaghetti noir* out of it from music by Ennio Morricone. I guess the film got so black that people were turned off."

1

2

3

4

5

(1–5) **JFK** was first conceived when Stone was stuck in an elevator in Havana, Cuba, with Ellen Ray, the publisher of a magazine called *Covert Intelligence*, in 1986. "These Communist elevators never work, so we're stuck and she was bending my ear for half an hour about the Kennedy assassination. Eventually I read the book and thought it was a great detective story. Purely on that level I thought it would make an exciting movie, but then we took it to other levels. I brought on Zach Sklar, who had been Jim Garrison's editor, to give me the real depth of what could have happened, because Jim had written a lot more. So I grafted these stories of Deeley Plaza, Oswald and Mr X on the movie."

JFK: "The script for **JFK** was so confusing with so many flashbacks that in the first draft [Warner Bros.] couldn't understand a thing. So I took it back, took all the flashbacks out as much as I could and gave it back to them, and they liked it and they went ahead with it. And then in the editing process we put them back in plus about 50 per cent more to give it a new style. We were going crazy at certain points in the editing because it was becoming so chaotic."

Some directors may put 20, 40 or 75 per cent of themselves into the movie but are under the illusion that it's 100 per cent. I don't put 100 per cent, I'm sure, but I certainly try to put the scope of all my feelings about the subject, and people often criticise my films for being overheated, but they wouldn't be what they are if they didn't have that passion behind them.

Stone worked with cinematographer Robert Richardson 11 times, although the two have recently parted ways. "We got a divorce in a way. There was definitely love there between us, but he was becoming increasingly critical of the work. He wants me to make **Alexander the Great** every time out, and I see nothing wrong with doing **U Turn** or **Any Given Sunday**, which may not be about assassinations, but they're nice because they fulfil other functions in our society."

biography

The prolific Ken Loach is one of Europe's premiere talents; a consistent ground-breaker and eminently gifted film-maker. His gut-wrenchingly authentic portraits of working-class life in the UK and elsewhere are redolent of documentaries but are far more dramatically powerful. Loach joined the BBC as a trainee director in 1963. His trademark documentary-style approach to drama first became searingly evident in **Cathy**

ken loach

Come Home, also made for TV in 1966, and he achieved widespread acclaim for his first two theatrical features **Poor Cow** (1967) and the heartbreaking **Kes** (1969). During the '70s and '80s he worked primarily for TV, making only the occasional feature film. A renewed vigour for cinema began with **Hidden Agenda** in 1990 about American human rights activists investigating abuses in Belfast, and continued with a trio of memorable dramas set in contemporary Britain: **Riff-Raff** (1991); **Raining Stones** (1993); and **Ladybird Ladybird** (1994). Using relatively unknown actors and an improvisational technique, Loach consistently achieves a truthfulness rare in contemporary cinema. His Spanish Civil War epic **Land and Freedom** (1995) seamlessly applied traditional Loach values to a period setting, as did **Carla's Song** (1996), partly set in Nicaragua in the late '80s, and **Bread and Roses** (2000), based on the Justice for Janitors strike in L.A. in 1990. But Loach kept returning to more traditional ground with his multi-award-winning character study **My Name is Joe** (1998) and **The Navigators** (2001). He is currently in production on **Sweet Sixteen** (2002).

interview

I didn't really see a film and think, "I want to do that". I directed in the theatre and then got a job in TV, so it gradually took me over. I had a sense of what a director was from working with different directors, most of whom weren't terribly good, and from doing things myself, which were pretty awful. So slowly I realised what all the bad things were and tried to improve on them. TV and films have more in common than not. You are trying to understand what the character and relationship and central ideas are that you're dealing with, and trying to explore them and find how to put an actor in touch with what he wants and what he has to do. Similarly, when I started I did what the cameramen told me to do because they knew how to work the camera, and I didn't. I watched what they did as routine and decided what I would've liked them to do, and then worked with good cameramen who were on my wavelength, and learned about it through them.

Filming is basically arranging for something to happen in front of a camera, so the question is how to make that realistic. Part of that is withdrawing all the technicalities of

1

2

3

(1–4) **Land and Freedom**: Loach's quest for truthful reactions occasionally means rewriting whole scenes. For example, in the final and crucial scene of **Land and Freedom** (4), where the militia is ordered to lay down its arms and Blanca (Rosana Pastor) is killed, Loach found that should he go with the script as it was, the dramatic power of the scene would be nullified. "According to the script originally, the regular army turns up and points their guns at the militia and in the script, the militia stays and argues. When we started shooting it, the moment the army pointed their guns, the militia just fled and disappeared behind bushes and down trenches. We had three cameras pointed at them, and suddenly there was nothing in the shot because they had all gone. So at the end of the first day on that scene, we went away and scratched our heads and realised that that reaction was bound to be right. So we had to change what the army did so that it didn't prompt that response. Their own instincts told me to change that scene. When you write the script, you can't always foresee someone's response. On set, I have to go with the actors' instincts. That's the most valuable thing you've got."

4

(5–6) **Bread and Roses**: Loach says that, while the film was more expensive than usual, it was still made without spending too much. "If we're shooting on location, we want to work as much as possible with local people, so if you're around them spending fortunes, they think you're there to be ripped off. It's better to work without ostentation. It's a much more human way to work. When we shot **Bread and Roses** in L.A., we went down in some people's estimation because we had such a small set of vans!" (6) Loach filming on location in L.A.

1

2

3

4

5

(1–5) The success of **Ladybird Ladybird** depended on who Loach would cast in the lead role of Maggie Conlan, a single mother fighting with Social Services to keep her children. He found Crissy Rock, a stand-up comic and singer ("more like Tina Turner than Edith Evans"), to play the part and, as his film-making technique dictates, Rock was kept in the dark as to the many crises her character would undergo until it came to shoot them. "She thought it was going to be the story of a woman who had a tough past and who has a happy ending when she meets the right man, so each time I came to give her a new scene, she couldn't believe it. When you first think of it, the hardest part is imagining how you are going to recreate that situation. How on earth can you get that monumental emotional strength? I suppose actors are like ships, and you have to guide them through rocky straits and narrow channels without them grounding. I didn't tell Crissy what to do, but showed her the path she might follow. And if the preparations are right, her instinct will lead her to respond in the way that will be true."

film-making as far as possible, so that people can just relate to each other and not to the equipment around them. You take away the impediments in order to make it credible. That means you don't shine lights in their eyes; you don't use a wide lens so you don't have to be too close, and position the sound in as unobtrusive a way as possible; you supplement natural light rather than lighting the room artificially. Natural light is, I think, usually more sympathetic. The cameraman also helps you read the performances. I learnt a lot from Chris Menges, with whom I worked for 20 years. He has a painter's attitude to light; he doesn't see objects, he sees light. Secondly, he would talk about the performances and what was emerging from the scene, the core of what was happening, and he would take delight in the way you could catch it directly. The cameraman I work with now, Barry Ackroyd, is also very talented and is equally engaged in the content of the film. We actually talk about the film as it's emerging.

This relationship is essential with the designer, Martin Johnson who is another long-time collaborator, and the cameraman. We will have a basic strategy for each scene. I'll have a plan scribbled on my script, and then I'll talk about it based on that. I would never storyboard: if you're just animating drawings that are fixed, the thing is already dead. The actors should have the space to develop a scene. Occasionally we cast people who have not acted before. Everyone's an actor really. The important thing is to find the people who can recreate the fictional events in front of the camera, and if you believe in them and you want to watch them – they're funny when they're meant to be funny, they touch you if they're sad – then it doesn't really make a difference if they've acted before or not. Our audition process is fairly extensive because we have to put the actors in

situations similar to when they'll be filmed. If they can get through those, they can do the film. For example, for **The Navigators**, which is set on the railways in South Yorkshire, we needed to find people from that area. I find that people who are entertainers – comics, singers – often have a vigour and humour that is true and authentic. Of the gang of six or seven we cast in **The Navigators**, about half were entertainers and half were actors. And that's quite a good combination. They each give a lot to each other.

When we are preparing and casting, the writer and I will have been through draft after draft of the script and tested it from every angle. What's the story? Is it worth telling? Does it have implications beyond the narrative? We work it over and scrutinise every scene. I have another old friend, Roger Smith, who is brilliant at this. We don't show the actors the script. It unfolds bit by bit. They might not know what's going to happen at the end, but they should know everything about the character, their past history and circumstances.

When I did TV, the read-through was often the best performance the actors gave, and the more you worked and directed it the less good they got. They became more studied, tricksy and less spontaneous. The camera sees through it.

I think one generalisation you can make is that however good the actor is, surprise is the hardest thing to do. There's a scene in **Bread and Roses**, for example, in which one sister hears something about the other sister's past and it just destroys her. Obviously I didn't want her to know what that secret was until we were shooting, so I didn't give her that part of the script. It didn't matter so much what she said as a response, it was the effect it had on her that was important. I think her response is quite genuine. There's nothing worse for actors than worrying whether they'll be able to cry or break down convincingly. It becomes paralysing, but if they just respond to the situation, it takes the pressure off completely.

It's very important to me to shoot in sequence. When you shoot a scene out of order, and a critical thing has happened in-between that you haven't filmed yet, you haven't explored it yet, so the actors don't know how they've emerged from it. You can't learn anything new emotionally in shooting the scene if you've already shot what comes after it. Control of the shooting schedule is definitely one of the most important things for a director.

The first thing you look for in an actor is do they listen and do they reflect back in a true way? Because the most important thing of all is not acting, it's reacting. One of the first things I look for in auditions is true responses. I do some preparation with actors. This is about establishing the relationships between the characters when the film starts, and knowing how their character spends their day. If they've got a job, they need to have some understanding of that job. We do a few scenes before the film starts, recreating a critical event which took place before the film begins, or if there's a married couple, a few scenes to see what kind of couple they are and how they function. Just by improvisation, they will have an emotional memory of the event so they've actually been through it in some way and can refer back to it when we're doing the film.

I will have worked out a basic plan for the scene which I hope will match the actors' instincts. When we're shooting a scene, I usually put it in the form of a question: "Where would you go?", "What would you do?", and with a bit of luck, they'll do what I anticipate, and if they don't, then I'll perhaps rearrange the room so that they'll go to a place where the light will be good, rather than somewhere where it won't. It's like digging a trench for a stream. You arrange the thing so that the actors will instinctively do what you want them to do. You make the actors the experts. We try to keep a good atmosphere on the set, which is very important. A bad atmosphere is uncreative. If the actors are really having to sweat and strain, they're probably doing something wrong. You want a certain tension and level of adrenaline, so it shouldn't be so easy that it's boring, but the excitement should come out of the work that you're doing, not out of any difficulties they're having.

You need a very good first assistant-director, and you need to be able to delegate. Ultimately you've got to be in control without it looking as though you're in control. A part of that is casting the crew like you would the actors, because the mix of personalities is really important. On one occasion we had a first assistant who was very aggressive, and we had to say goodbye to him because it was so destructive. There's no special treatment for the actors. Everyone is in the same queue at lunchtime. In my experience, if you take away those silly privileges, people are much happier. It's much better that they all just muck in.

I don't look at rushes much because I know more or less what we've shot. I think it's very damaging to work with monitors. We have a little postage-stamp-sized one on the side of the camera for the focus puller to be able to check the camera's movement, because often the camerawork isn't fixed, but that's it. If everybody can see a monitor, the intimacy of the relationship between the cameraman and the actor is lost.

1   2   3

(1–2) Loach enjoys a long-term partnership with writer Paul Laverty, with whom he has worked on **My Name is Joe**, among others. Laverty had met some female social workers whom he respected, out of which the film emerged. "We wanted to do a story about some of the relationships they have, so it was Paul's idea to involve a man burdened by being a former alcoholic, so really it became the story of two people who dare not make themselves vulnerable to a relationship." (3–4) **Poor Cow** was Loach's first theatrical film. In it, Carol White plays a woman in an abusive marriage who falls for her husband's best friend (Terence Stamp) while he's in prison. For Loach, although the bleak subject matter was characteristic, **Poor Cow** marked his last flirtation with name casts.

4

1

2

3

4

5

Loach was a prolific TV drama director who had had a hit in 1967 with **Poor Cow**, but his fame started to spread only after **Kes** was released in 1969 (1–3). Screened at Cannes in 1970, and indeed beginning a long association between Loach and Cannes, **Kes** was an adaptation of Barry Hines' novel 'Kestrel for a Knave', and featured an extraordinarily naturalistic performance by teenager David Bradley as Billy Casper, a young working-class schoolboy whose only escape from the prospects of a limited future is a kestrel which he finds and trains. The film, shot in unadorned colour by Chris Menges, remains a milestone in socially conscious film-making. (4–5) Loach with cameramen on set.

I think the job is quite physically demanding. You're projecting all the time. Every day a new scene has to succeed. Frequently I feel anxious about whether it's working or not, but one of the best things about shooting quickly is that you gain speed. That's when people's adrenaline starts working and they work much better. The performances are physically better than if you have a day to do a shot, in which case nobody can get motivated. Those disciplines of shooting quickly can generate energy and be very constructive, and whether the whole thing works or not is dependent on energy.

I've worked with the same editor, Jonathan Morris, for the last 20 years. We don't start to cut until we've finished shooting, and then we just piece it together shot-by-shot and make sure that we're open to the rhythm of each shot. So we start with the shaping of individual scenes to begin with and then shape the film as a whole after that.

When we're cutting, the writer and the actors will often pop in to see us, which I think is a good thing because it means it's more than just a job they've done and forgotten. You want that sort of loyalty and commitment from the start and, of course, you must give it in return. It's also nice for Jonathan because editors can sometimes be isolated from the rest of the team.

We're reconciled to the fact that our films will never be big multiplex material, because the multiplex has got a very narrow menu. When I was young, there were cinemas playing French and Italian films, even in the smaller towns. Now that's not the case, and the kind of films we make don't fit in with what the multiplexes think the audiences want to see. Competition, of course, doesn't lead to choice, it leads to a lack of choice. Films tend to belong to one type or another.

But still there seems to be a core audience in Italy, France and Spain that sees them, so that's OK.

biography

Along with Reiner Werner Fassbinder, Wim Wenders pioneered New German Cinema and has remained its most original and distinctive voice, creating a series of aesthetically beautiful studies of alienation and wandering, which are both mesmerising and disturbing. Educated at the University of Film and TV in Munich, Wenders made his feature debut in 1970 with **Summer in the City**, followed in

wim wenders

1971 by **The Goalkeeper's Fear of the Penalty Kick (Die Angst des Tormanns beim Elfmeter)**. He achieved international acclaim with his "road movie" trilogy: **Alice in the Cities (Alice in den Städten**, 1974); **Wrong Movement (Falsche Bewegung**, 1975); and **Kings of the Road (Im Lauf der Zet**, 1976). Having established his own company Road Movies Filmproduktion in 1976, he made his first English-language film **The American Friend (Der Amerikanische Freund)** in 1977. He returned to the road movie with lyrical effect in 1984 with **Paris, Texas**, following it with his black-and-white existential opus **Wings of Desire** (1987). His films since then have become more complex, ambitious and expensive with differing results: the futuristic epic **Until the End of the World** (1991); **Faraway, So Close (In Weiter Ferne, so Nah!**, 1993); **Lisbon Story** (1995); the thriller **The End of Violence** (1997); and **The Million Dollar Hotel** (1999). Ironically, music documentary **Buena Vista Social Club** (1999) brought him his biggest success of the '90s. He is currently preparing another road movie co-written with Sam Shepard.

interview

I never intended to become a film-maker. And I never saw movies like other film-makers did, when I was growing up. I mean I liked movies, but I never understood what a director was. That came much later, when I was living in Paris, trying to become a painter. I was poor and it was cold and I would go to the Cinémathèque [Francaise] in the afternoons to see movies, mainly because it was a warm place that only cost one franc per screening. The programme started in the afternoon and went through the evening until midnight, and at weekends the last show would be at two in the morning. The first thing I saw was an entire Anthony Mann retrospective. Later there was also a John Ford retrospective and a Fritz Lang retrospective. I was seeing an average of five or six films a day. If you paid for the first show and went to the toilet between shows, and waited until the theatre was filling up again, you could go back in without buying another ticket, so you could get away with spending only a franc for five movies.

I saw Japanese movies, German movies, American movies with Arabic subtitles – whatever Henri Langlois [the founder

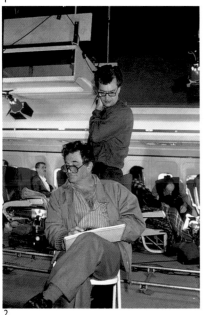

7

8

(1–9) "In **Wings of Desire**, black and white was the privileged view and colour the normal or 'vulgar' view. People would see in colour, but angels would see the privileged way. I used to feel that way when I was making those films: in black and white you would somehow see the essence of things, and in colour their surface. However, I haven't done a black-and-white film in some time. In my photography, I am strictly sticking to colour. I feel one can only be either a black-and-white photographer or a colour photographer. Berlin was entirely suited to being represented in black and white, I thought. It was much more photogenic that way, or rather, black and white corresponded to its soul more than colour did."
(2–3) Wenders on the set of **Wings of Desire**.

9

of the Cinémathèque] could get his hands on. I think I saw 1,500 films in that time, a crash course of the history of cinema. Then I bought books of film history to try and place all the films I'd seen, and then I started making notes about the experience of those movies. I slowly realised I was moving away from painting and in the direction of cinema. I was then heavily impressed by what was called "The New American Underground" at the time – [Andy] Warhol, Michael Snow, directors who were also painters – and so it seemed to me there was an interesting crossroads between painting and film-making. After that period at the Cinémathèque, I applied to the first film school in Germany which opened in Munich. Out of 1,000 applications, they chose 20, and I was one of them. Fassbinder had also applied, but they refused him, which was lucky for him, because it made him so angry that he started making movies right away, while us poor suckers sat there in the film school doing stupid courses.

I still never thought that I would become a director at this point. I had strictly applied because I thought I was going to take the writing more seriously, and there was this idea in my head which tied painting and movies and writing together. The first time I actually thought I was a director was after I'd made my fourth film already, **Alice in the Cities**. After my third film, **Scarlet Letter**, I was very discouraged. It was sort of an academic picture, and I figured that if I was going to go on with this film-making business, I would have to prove to myself that I could do something that nobody else could, or else I would just have to stop doing it. And **Alice in the Cities** turned out to be the proof that I had something to say, and that film-making was worth continuing with. For me that film represented my very own invention of what I wanted to do in movies. The three previous films had been accidents, I felt.

Alice was personal and unique; the story was all mine, and I had turned it into imagery of my own as well. And for the first time there was no rupture between my initial desire for a movie and what it turned out to be. It was actually pretty much as I had envisioned it. There was a unity between conception, realisation and result that made me feel I had actually controlled the process.

In those early movies – **Summer in the City**, **Alice in the Cities**, **Wrong Movement**, **Kings of the Road** and **The American Friend** – the topic of alienation ran through them all. The American reviewers summed them up under "angst and alienation", and I called those reviews the "Triple-A-reviews": "Angst, Alienation and America". I never thought those topics were really at the core of my films. My notion was that my films all dealt with a search for something that I couldn't quite define. All I knew was that it wasn't there and had to be reinvented. You see I was born into post-war Germany. My whole thinking came very much from the perspective of somebody who had to put it all back together from scratch. And my films are also driven by the desire to leave my country behind. So there was a lot of travelling. I like to shoot on the road, and so I called my company Road Movies Filmproduktion. I feel very comfortable when I am moving. I can work so much better on the road than at home.

In the beginning, I was totally obsessed with "framing". It was the most important aspect of the whole film-making process for me. I would design all shots in advance, and I would have my layout ready in the morning, when I would come on set. I would know exactly which shots I would do and then the scenes had to fit into that concept. That very exact notion of framing was my security blanket. Later I started to feel more

2

Wenders' films have been inextricably linked with their evocative music, whether it be Ry Cooder's melancholic score for **Paris, Texas** or Jürgen Knieper's for **Wings of Desire**, or the use of rock tracks. (2) Nick Cave and The Bad Seeds actually play in **Wings of Desire** and Lou Reed acted in **Faraway, So Close** (1). "From the very beginning, music has been important to me. The title of my first feature-film, **Summer in the City**, came from a Lovin' Spoonful song. Sometimes I feel the most precious moment in the whole film-making process – from conception to location scouting to casting to shooting, editing and mixing – is the moment you see a scene for the first time with its music. Rock and roll has been very important in my films, as in **Kings of the Road** and in **The American Friend** which has that whole tribute to The Kinks in it. 17 bands contributed to the soundtrack for **Until the End of the World**, and the soundtrack to **Lisbon Story** featured the music of Madredeus, which was the recording which made them famous."

directing

(1–2) Stills from Wenders' 1993 follow-up to **Wings of Desire**, **Faraway, So Close**. Wenders' first long-term collaborator and cinematographer was Robby Müller, who worked on 12 Wenders projects. "In terms of lighting, I give my directors of photography all the freedom in the world. In terms of angles and frames, I've always set those myself. Most D.P.s are happy with that, because they have their hands full with the lighting and the operating anyway. I prefer to work with D.P.s who operate themselves, although Henri Alekan [who shot **Wings of Desire** and **The State of Things**] and Phedon Papamichael [who shot **The Million Dollar Hotel**] didn't. Robby was always fine with me setting the frame. And sometimes he'd come up with an angle I had not foreseen." (3) Wenders with cinematographer Pascal Rabaud, shooting **The End of Violence**.

and more, though, that it was a trap if I knew too well what I was going to do before I'd even start to work with the actors. The last film I made with that attitude was **The American Friend**. I only let my security blanket go after I directed a play for the first time, 'Across the Villages' by my friend Peter Handke. Working with actors on stage was such a different experience. There was a total absence of framing, for once. I learned a lot from it and the next film I did after that, **Paris, Texas**, was done without any drawings or preconceived notions about set-ups and framing. That was a conscious choice I made before the film.

On that film, I just went to work every morning without the slightest idea how I was going to shoot. I would just start working with the actors on the scene, and only when we felt comfortable with it, I would start to develop a "decoupage": where to put the camera, and how to cut from wide shots to close-ups or other angles. It was a much more flexible approach. And addictive. For the first time the actors became the principals. The actors and the story were the heroes, not the style or the look. Before, style and look had had a priority over the story. On **Paris, Texas**, I took the story and its emotions and the actors more seriously than the look of the film. The theatre experience had opened me up to a less formalistic approach to film-making and **Paris, Texas** profited a lot from that. My cinematographer Robby Müller would come onto the set in the morning and wouldn't know what the first set-up would be, and we wouldn't know how many set-ups we had to do that day. I would just come and talk with the actors about what the scene was all about and what the emotions of the scene were, and then we'd walk around and see how and where we could do it. Then we'd try to play it, and only after that would I sit down with Robby and

discuss how to shoot it. That whole process was much more from the guts than from the brain. It felt pretty risky at first, but so much more connected.

Sam Shepard and I had not written a complete screenplay for **Paris, Texas**. We had only written the first half for good. The second half we knew was baloney, and we only presented it to show a full script. Our plan was that Sam would be with me while we were shooting, and that as we went along we would get to know the characters and our story better. We would shoot the film in chronological order, and when we'd get to the middle, Sam and I could then continue writing it. However, the film got postponed a couple of times and when we finally started shooting, Sam had a commitment to be in a film called **Country** with Jessica Lange in Minnesota. So he was up north and I was in Texas. Fax machines didn't exist yet. I had half a script, and when we came to the end of those written pages, the whole shoot came to a grinding halt. I sent everybody home and in the next two weeks wrote the second half. Kit Carson [who has a co-writing credit on the film] helped me a bit with the structure, and finally I was able to send Sam a layout of 20 pages of how I imagined the end of the story. And then Sam would call me every night with the scene for the next day. He would read it out to me over the phone and I would write it down. He basically dictated the dialogue, and the next morning I would photocopy it and we would shoot it during the day. In the evening we were back on the telephone.

The original ending was totally different, but then I had this idea about the peepshow, and again interrupted shooting for three days to write the outline for the new ending. Then Sam actually wrote the dialogue for that ending over one weekend.

It was 30 pages long. I guess taking the dictation on it was the longest phone call I ever made. And then we had the entire peepshow section to shoot which consisted of two long scenes. Harry Dean [Stanton] and Nastassja [Kinski] had two days and two nights to learn it. We liked the two scenes so much that we decided not to shoot them piece by piece, but each of them in one go, as if they were a stage performance of two acts of a play.

I have a very sharpened sense of place. Most of my films were initiated by the desire to explore a certain place, and some of them, like **Lisbon Story**, **The Million Dollar Hotel** or **Paris, Texas** have been called by the place itself. It's not just that places matter to me, it's the idea that stories are specific to certain places. I want the place to be so tightly connected to the story that I know in my heart that this story can only happen here. I think I have a good sense of how to approach a place and how to represent it so that as you follow the scene, you know exactly where you are. That's very important to me – to be able to let the audience enter a place and understand where they are. I think I learned that from watching the films of Anthony Mann or Howard Hawks.

With **Wings of Desire**, I wanted to make a film in my own country after an absence of eight years in America. Coming back to Berlin was a rediscovery. More than anything I have ever done, **Wings of Desire** was made strictly from the guts. There was never a written script whatsoever. The film was made like you would write a poem, very much improvised. I wasn't so radical as to shoot entirely without a plan, though. There was a wall in my office with ideas and scenes and images and hunches pinned to it, and at night, I would stand before the wall with Claire Denis, my assistant, and we'd figure out what we would do the next day. Rather than putting pressure on you, I feel, this frees you up like nothing else. Scripts put much more pressure on me.

The story in **Wings of Desire** is so flimsy anyway: these angels are watching over people, and one of them falls in love and wants to become a human being. It's a fairy tale more than anything else. I never thought in terms of story; I always thought in terms of moods and situations. Each scene was a sort of poetic entity. I never knew exactly where the ideas came from. It was a deeply subconscious process, and I wanted to keep it that way.

The film looks very rich, and that is due to the fact that Henri Alekan shot it. He is the all-time champion, the master of the black-and-white craft. The actors were very adventurous and ready to work on a day-by-day basis. The two angel characters didn't have any biography or their lives to worry about. For once we didn't need any motivations or any psychology! I wanted to revisit Berlin later to make **Faraway, So Close**, because it was no longer the city that we had shot **Wings of Desire** in. It had changed more radically probably than any other city in the last century in such a short period of time. At first, I didn't think at all about using the same characters and started to write something about taxi drivers and children and firemen, and all sorts of people travelling between the two halves of Berlin. But then, the more I travelled through the city myself, the more I realised that the only appropriate approach would be to see it through the same eyes of the angels again. So I considered bringing these characters back, almost against my will or against better knowledge. Sequels are such a scary thing. I just never thought of **Faraway** as a sequel, though, more as a continuation.

2

3

(1) Wenders' bold visual style in **The End of Violence** not only references Edward Hopper's painting 'Nighthawks' in this scene – which is actually the shooting of a movie within a movie – but showed one of the starkest views of L.A. ever seen on screen. "I tried to find a look for the city that would enhance the idea that there's always something behind what you see, and that the city is only a front for a real city behind the façade. In the film, that real world is the world of the gardeners, and the principal character's world is built on the fact that you only need the façade of the city." Wenders shot much of the film at the Observatory in Griffith Park, most famous for featuring in Nicholas Ray's **Rebel Without a Cause**. Wenders, of course, knew Ray and had collaborated with him on **Lightning Over Water** in 1980. "I love the Observatory, and the hill that leads up to it. Sometimes you have this blurred vision of the city covered in mist or smog. Sometimes you can see to the ocean; sometimes you can't even see the first street. It's the evasiveness of L.A., I guess." (2–3) Wenders' freewheeling 1991 futuristic opus **Until the End of the World** was shot around the world in Japan, China, Russia, Germany, Portugal, France, Italy and, most crucially, Australia. "The entire project started when I discovered the Aboriginal culture in Australia. Each of the places in the film is a place I have affection for and that I wanted to shoot in. Each of those places inspired the writing of its part in the film." (3) Wenders on location.

directing

1

2

3

(1–3) The powerful peepshow scene (1) which ends **Paris, Texas** was shot like a one-act play, with a full 1,000-feet magazine which would run for ten minutes. "If there was a blunder in the middle, we just cut and started again from the beginning. I had never worked like this before. We must have done it about 20 times. It was the biggest expense of the whole film. It drove the production manager crazy. He couldn't understand why, if we had a good half, we didn't start from the middle and just do the other half. He had to keep re-ordering film. And I kept insisting we shoot it only as a complete text. We only stopped shooting when we had it perfectly in one take."

I've made several documentaries or documentary-like movies that I rather called diaries or journals, like **Tokyo-Ga** and **Notebook on Cities and Clothes** or **Reverse Angle**. They are explorations of places or professions. **Buena Vista Social Club** started just like that, as an idea to make a personal account of the encounter with these musicians and of my first encounter with the city of Havana. I didn't have an aesthetic plan or smart approach to how to show them. I started shooting the day I arrived and tried to discover who these musicians were whose music I'd loved so much, ever since Ry Cooder had given me a cassette of a rough mix, when he had come back from Havana the first time.

The whole fun of the film was that there was no preparation and that it was done on a day-to-day basis. I first imagined I'd spend a month in Havana, come home and edit it. But when we came back from Havana, the possibility opened up that these musicians' paths would cross in Amsterdam and that it might be possible to bring this non-existent band together in one place and have them play for real, for one time only. I wanted to be there, of course, so we got ready for a second leg of our shoot.

The concert then actually happened, and I shot for another week in Amsterdam, the two concerts and four days of rehearsal, and all of a sudden I had two very distinct parts to the film which I didn't know how to fit together. The concert was such a success, and became almost legendary overnight, and as a result the remote chance appeared that the Cubans might actually get visas to give one performance at Carnegie Hall! I couldn't possibly miss out on this one, so of course I got another crew together and went to New York and that gave me the third chapter. In the end, I had over 100 hours of material and spent almost a year trying to put the puzzle together. There had been no structure planned for such complex footage. We had to find the story that would tie it all together. That story had in fact happened in front of our eyes. A story bigger than life, almost a fairy tale: the incredible path of these artists from oblivion to world stardom. The whole process, from A to Z, never felt like I was actually working, because their joy of making music was so contagious, that it always felt like a sheer pleasure to be there with them.

I think the most privileged moments in movie-making are when the work feels as close as possible to making music or poetry. And sometimes shooting can get very close to that indeed. I recently finished producing a documentary by a young American film-maker, Dominic DeJoseph, who followed the making of **The Million Dollar Hotel** and the making of the music for it, and he concentrated on the links between the film and its music. In their best moments, the two have a lot in common. The film is called **One Dollar Diary**.

When I was shooting the musicians at work in **Buena Vista Social Club**, we almost became members of the band, and the way we tried to move around them was as if our cameras were also musical instruments. And **Wings of Desire** was as close I think as you can get to poetry, considering you are working with the very organised machinery, equipment and logistics of film-making to live out the unorganised intentions of a poet.

One of the true originals of world cinema, David Lynch emerged with such a distinctive film-making voice, in ground-breaking classics such as **Eraserhead**, **Blue Velvet** and the TV series *Twin Peaks*, that he spawned both an adjective ("Lynchian") and a thousand imitators. With a passionate eye for the quirks of human nature, a penchant for abstractions, a bold and inventive visual sense and effortless storytelling

david lynch

131

skills, he has produced a wildly varied canon of work. Films range from the black-and-white period drama **The Elephant Man** (1980) to science-fiction epic **Dune** (1984) – from which he removed his name when final cut was denied him on the TV version – to beautifully tender character study **The Straight Story** (1999). Originally planning to be a painter, he started experimenting with film when studying at the Pennsylvania Academy of Fine Arts, where he made short films **The Alphabet** (1968) and **The Grandfather** (1970). His first feature, the nightmarish black-and-white "symphony" **Eraserhead** was made between 1971 and 1976 and became a cult hit when it was released. It opened the doors for Lynch to make **The Elephant Man** with producer Mel Brooks. Among Lynch's other films are **Wild at Heart** (1990) which won the Palme d'Or at Cannes, **Twin Peaks: Fire Walk with Me** (1992), a prequel of sorts to the TV series, **Lost Highway** (1997), an ambitious, multi-layered piece, and **Mulholland Drive** (2001), a feature reconfigured from a cancelled TV pilot for which Lynch shared the Best Direction prize at Cannes in 2001.

There's no conventional way to do anything. There are films that fall into a pattern we are used to, but every story is different so every film has got different problems, and they've got to be solved. I don't even think that Hollywood has one way, although generally speaking money drives the boat. It's a business for a lot of people, and a good film for them is a film that makes money. Some of my films have made money, and it's a beautiful thing when a film breaks even because no-one has lost out, but money should never be the reason you do it.

I never thought about film when I was young, I wanted to be a painter from about the age of 15, and I ended up at the Pennsylvania Academy of Fine Arts. That was like a little golden age in my mind. I painted sometimes in this big room where everybody had a little area, and that's where this revelation happened. I heard sounds and saw my painting move, which got me interested in animation. From then on, that's all I wanted to do. My first film was a one-minute animated film which was looped to the sound of a siren and I built a sculptured screen for it to be projected on.

directing

1

2

3

4

(1–4) **The Elephant Man**: Lynch with John Hurt on location (1). Lynch was given his second feature by comic actor and film-maker Mel Brooks, who hired him to direct the film. "He was like a knight in shining armour, a saint, a powerhouse of protection. I can't explain it. The guy was solid gold. It just doesn't make sense that he put me on it. It's a Victorian drama and I'd never been to London. I've got one strange feature to my name and I'm off to work with Sir John Gielgud. But when I heard the words **The Elephant Man**, a thing occurred in my brain and the next instant I said, 'that's the film I have to do'." Describing the film as "a traditional costume drama with some curve balls in it", Lynch shot on location in a derelict hospital in London where, he says, he immediately felt an affinity for the 19th-century England setting he was recreating. "Standing in that hospital, I felt like I had been born and raised in that time in London. It became second-hand to me. I caught a feel of it, just like you want actors to catch the feel of things. From that point on, I felt like I knew it like Tony Hopkins knew it. I love industry, and the film was set in the time when industry was developing, and so it was a combination of flesh, humans and machines in the air at the time, which was a little bit evocative of **Eraserhead**."

By the time I made **Eraserhead**, I'd made three short films and had been accepted into the Center for Advanced Film Studies at the American Film Institute, where I was taught by the greatest film teacher ever to walk the earth, Frank Daniel. I was film illiterate in many ways, but so much of film is common sense and intuition, and stories are basically ideas translated into the language of film, so in some ways you don't have to know anything to make a film, you just have to understand the process of translation. Frank enlivened the components of film for me like editing, sound, music, acting, sequence, repetition of shapes and so on. The same rules that exist in any medium exist in film, only maybe a little bit more. He made me notice the parts and how they relate to the whole, and helped me with the structure of a feature.

To me film is painting and taking still photos and time thrown in together. It's the ultimate art, but within that you can get excited about so many other things. It opens up a beautiful world. Every medium has its beauty and every medium is infinitely deep. You can go deep, deep into still photography and have an experience that you would never have in film. So that's not a lesser thing than film, but of course film has the advantage of being able to move!

There are certain rules in film, but then again there are no rules. It's like a chair – some chairs work really great with three legs, but they still have to be comfortable to sit on. Similarly, there are lots of ways to work within a feature film structure and you arrange the number of things you can do within that, which is probably infinite. Again, most of it depends on the story. If you follow the story, then a structure emerges. It's not an intellectual thing – it's more intuition, and in my mind intuition is emotion and intellect working

together. It's almost a knowing. Ideas direct you, and ideas come from who knows where. They're like electricity because they pop into your mind like a spark and that spark is like a seed. Suddenly the whole scene or character or portion of the story is there. Bango, it's there and you know it instantly and it thrills your soul. You embrace that bad boy and hold tight, and never forget it because the whole thing is in that little idea. One night I was on *Twin Peaks* and we had just finished editing for the day and we were in the parking lot – me, the editor of the pilot Duwayne Dunham, and his assistant Brian – and it had been a sunny day but the sun was just setting and I was leaning against the hood of a car and it was really warm. It was beautiful to feel this warmth and bango, I started talking loud to Duwayne and the Man From Another Place In The Red Room came into my head. It just came in like that. I don't know why it occurred when it occurred, but it occurred.

In the old studio system, a guy would come in and throw a script on your desk and say, "that's your next picture, bud", and you'd read it and by reading it you'd catch ideas the same way that the writer caught ideas and arranged them into a story and words. Once you'd read the script, it came alive in your mind and you would translate what you felt and saw into film using the language of film, so it's not a script anymore. It has changed inevitably because ideas captured on the way fill out certain things. Nevertheless you stay true to the original thing because that's what you're hanging everything on.

I've been a writer on everything except **The Straight Story**. To me a script is not a finished product. The script is more like an indication, a blueprint – it's not the house. You can see the house in your mind's eye when you look at the blueprint, but eventually you're going to get the experience of

1

2

(1–3) Lynch describes working on his 1984 epic **Dune**, based on the novel by Frank Herbert, as "a nightmare – a beautiful nightmare but a nightmare nevertheless". The film was shot on eight sound stages at Churubusco in Mexico City. "The stages were filled twice with sets, so it was the equivalent of 16 sound stages filled to the brim with sets. Freddie Francis [the cinematographer] said we had to shoot as if we were on location as there was no room for anything. We shot the film over a year, six months principal photography and six months on models, special effects and miniatures."

3

Describing the backer of **Dune**, legendary producer Dino De Laurentiis as a "fantastic human being but horrible to work with if you don't have final cut", Lynch nevertheless again worked with the producer on his next film after **Dune**, his seminal **Blue Velvet** (4–9). This time, however, he had final cut. "He told me if I cut my salary in half and cut my budget in half, I could get final cut on **Blue Velvet**. I would have had my salary cut completely for that, and indeed he was true to his word and I had final cut." (2) Lynch with Raffaella De Laurentiis, Dino's daughter, who was producer on the film.

4

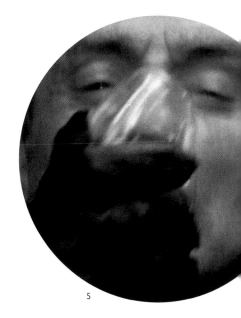

5

6

7

8

9

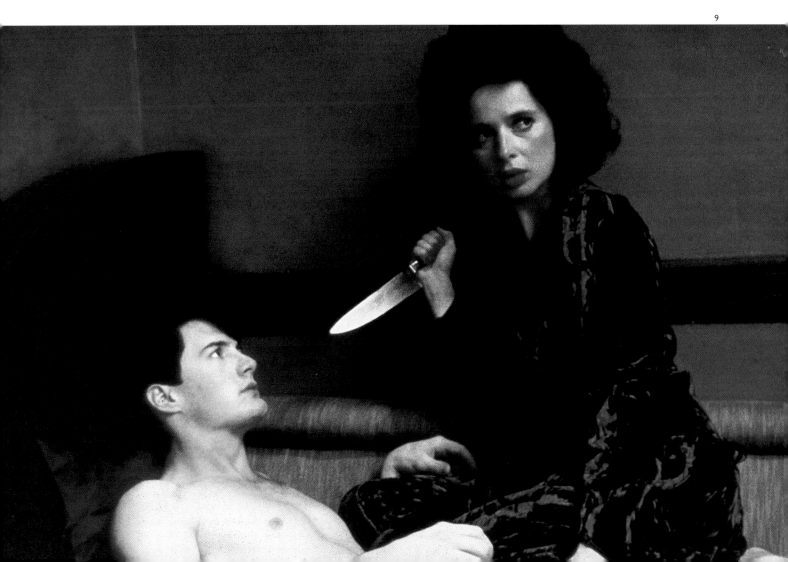

walking in there and you realise that the blueprint is nothing compared with the real thing.

When I'm casting, I try to get the person that fulfils the need of that role as perfectly as possible. Then you see that this person maybe isn't exactly the thing you wanted but even better. Willem Dafoe, for example, gave a flawless performance in **Wild at Heart**. He became this character of Bobby Peru so much, it was phenomenal. We talked, we rehearsed, but then he just made it his own and nailed it. The same with Dennis Hopper in **Blue Velvet**. He was perfect for the role and then the thing just lit on fire. When Frank comes in, you know it, you feel that it's right.

The film is always expanding, while staying true to the original, so in rehearsals, you're trying to get everybody to tune in with you into that same thing, and once everybody is tuned in, then you're moving along as one and that's the trick – then you have a chance of the whole thing staying together. When I start shooting, it's just a point of departure. You know what you want to get, but it's like at the beginning of the day you set out on a very thin glass bridge. At any moment the bridge could break and you'd fall to your death. Every time you capture something on film that you feel is correct, behind you it's starting to turn to steel, but you're still going through the day across this delicate but tender, fragile glass bridge. When you've finished your day it should be all steel, but the next day it's glass again.

I do rehearsals, but I prefer to get going in front of the camera because the sets or the location are there, the actors are there in costume and it's much more real. A lot has to be set up ahead of time and all those people who are setting up have to tune into your thing in order to get the right feel. When we are at the location, we talk and search for a mood that supports the story in this particular scene. The camera's got to drift in a certain way. The original idea dictates everything. Sometimes I use music so that the cameraman will move the camera in the right way. On **Lost Highway**, we played music during shooting and I heard music and dialogue, but the cinematographer Peter Deming only heard music through his headphones, so he moved the camera in a different way.

The more comfortable a set is, the better it is because actors go out on a limb more. It's so frightening to let go of yourself and take on another persona. It's dangerous. It can be a disaster but the more comfortable you are doing it, the better you are going to do it. I like things to feel safe for the actors and give them whatever they need to make that thing real.

Editing is a crucial process in film-making. As you go along, the film becomes more concrete and the path narrows but there are still many, many things one can do to make it feel correct and get yourself out of trouble. Never fall in love with a scene, they say, because you know that maybe it is going to end up on the floor. And then this scene you shot, almost because it was just there, now saves the whole film. So the process continues. If you change one thing, you'll change ten other things. You're looking for a balance and a feeling of correctness. There is a saying: keep your eye on the doughnut and not on the hole, so the doughnut is the story and the hole is the billion distractions and pressures. You just have to focus on the story. Even James Cameron has the same pressures with all that money. In fact, restrictions can sometimes help you, because you have an idea about how big your corral is. Some ideas come along which are beautiful

1

2

Whether it's John Merrick's death to the sound of Barber's 'Adagio for Strings' in **The Elephant Man**, Dorothy Vallens (Isabella Rossellini) warbling 'Blue Velvet' (page 135, 4), or the road trip of Sailor and Lula to the accompaniment of Chris Isaak's haunting song, 'Wicked Game', in **Wild at Heart** (1–3), music plays a central and memorable part in Lynch's films. "It has to have a very good reason for being, and it has to do some beautiful work in a scene to be included. Some music can actually ruin a scene. On the other hand, the right piece of music can elevate that scene. Like everything else, it's an experiment." Lynch works closely with Angelo Badalamenti, who scored **Blue Velvet**, **Wild at Heart**, **Twin Peaks: Fire Walk with Me**, **Lost Highway** and **The Straight Story**, as well as TV projects *Twin Peaks*, *Hotel Room* and *On the Air*, to "tune him in" to the project. "I talk to Angelo about certain things and he plays what I talk. I say no and talk again, he plays some more and eventually, sometimes very quickly, he'll start playing something that is so perfect that I say, 'that's it, Angelo', and he is on the right track." (1–2) Lynch with chief **Wild at Heart** protagonists – Nicholas Cage (Sailor) (1) and Laura Dern (Lula) (2).

3

(1–5) **Twin Peaks: Fire Walk with Me**: Lynch stayed closely involved in the TV series *Twin Peaks* for the first seven-episode season, but thereafter his obligations to **Wild at Heart** saw him entrust the second season to other hands. "I loved directing my episodes but you have to let go after a while. The other episodes sometimes veered away from what I thought was *Twin Peaks*, but still the corral was pretty big and they could go into this area and see some pigs, or over here to see some calves and it would all stay within *Twin Peaks*. It got a little out of balance, but there's not enough hours in the day to stay just on that, and we had great directors who did great stuff." As for the spin-off movie **Twin Peaks: Fire Walk with Me**, Lynch remains loyal to his vision despite a critical lambasting. "That's the way it goes. I felt that there was a black cloud which came over me at that time in the eyes of the world. Sometimes you go up and sometimes you go down. I happen to love that film." (3) Lynch himself acts in the movie.

4

5

1

2

4

5

3

(1–3) **Mulholland Drive**: After the success of *Twin Peaks*, Lynch re-teamed with US TV network ABC for a pilot called *Mulholland Drive* in 1997, but the network abandoned the film after it was shot, and Lynch sourced French financing to complete it as a theatrical feature. "The road from when you have the first idea to the time when it's released is one with many turns. This one had a few extra turns but it needed them. It was almost magical to me the way this started and turned and veered and almost went off a cliff and came back and began to metamorphose into what it is." **Mulholland Drive** premiered in competition at Cannes in 2001 and it won Lynch shared Best Director. (2) Lynch with Laura Harring and Naomi Watts, whose interchanging characters in the film are at the heart of the mystery. (3) Lynch on the set of the film.

(4–5) Perhaps one of Lynch's most unexpected movies was the lyrical and gentle **The Straight Story** starring Richard Farnsworth as Alvin Straight, a 73-year-old man who travels thousands of miles across country on a lawnmower, to reunite with his estranged and ailing brother. "I always said it was my most experimental film. There's very little to work with and at the same time a whole bunch to work with. The balance is different, that's all, so it was an experiment for me to find that balance in each scene and in the whole thing. It was a beautiful experiment and pretty minimal, but like a piece of music appears and disappears, it was critical to get the delicate scenes of emotion right. Emotion is an abstraction, nobody knows exactly how come you feel like crying at a certain point. Yet it's because of the parts being a certain way. It's like in music – a symphony starts and the start is critical: it can be beautiful, but it can't be so beautiful that it robs from something coming down the line. And that something coming down the line may be beautiful by itself, but not anywhere near as beautiful as it would be if it has all the things that lead up to it." Lynch describes the final scene of the film in which Alvin and his brother Lyle are reunited as a "trillion dollar moment. Maybe more than a trillion." (5) Lynch on location.

because they don't cost a fortune, and your mind goes to work solving problems within that corral.

You never know how people will react to a film when it's finished, which is the heartache of it and maybe the beauty too. You give up all control when a film is finished, which is horrible. In a way, that's part of the hole and not the doughnut.

In cinema, if everybody was true to their stories and themselves, then there would be many unique voices. Film is a tricky business, because you can't put a false overlay on something without people with half an ounce of feeling or intelligence smelling a rat. I can't do a Fellini picture and I shouldn't want to do a Fellini picture. Fellini should do Fellini pictures. That's why it was so beautiful to see what Kubrick was up to. You would look forward to the day his films opened to see what this guy was going to come up with next. They were true to themselves and their stories. There are certain stories that you can tell will possibly make more money in the marketplace than others, but if you fall in love with a story, you shouldn't think about that. It's like some girl whom you might not think would be so welcome when you bring her home, but you're in love and there's nothing you can do. You understand her and she understands you, and it doesn't matter what other people think.

I refuse to give explanations of any film I make. Film can be abstract and abstractions exist in everyday life and they give us a feeling, and our intuition goes to work, and we make sense of it for ourselves. It's said that audiences – and this is a really general statement and I'm not sure I believe it fully – may not trust themselves to figure out an abstraction unless it's explained to them, but they do figure it out even if they don't realise it. Everybody understands abstractions but sometimes they're a little fearful of them. Film does them so beautifully in its own language, often without words, and in fact words sometimes get in the way of some beautiful abstractions. You just have to surrender, let go. Watching a film is like standing in front of a painting. It's talking to you and it's about a circle from the screen to the viewer to the screen to the viewer. Once the circle starts rolling, the same film can be seen 100 different ways by 100 different people. That's why I refuse to explain my films. If you read a book by some famous dead author, you can't ask him what he meant by certain things. He started his book in a certain way and told his story in his way and finished it. It occupied his life for a time and now it exists and that's really all that's necessary. Nothing needs to be added, or he would have added it.

Do I have a favourite of my films? No. Let me say they're like children. Each child is different and each has their special qualities and you love them all and they're little rascals. You can't pick a favourite and if you had one, you shouldn't say, because it would hurt the feelings of the others.

biography

James Ivory and his partners, producer Ismail Merchant and screenwriter Ruth Prawer Jhabvala, have carved out and maintained a unique niche within film – a cottage industry of intelligent, consistently successful productions which they generate and raise the finance for independently from bases in New York, London and Paris. Although most famous for his impressive canon of literary adaptations, the range of films

james ivory

directed by Ivory is intriguingly wide. His first feature, **The Householder** in 1963, a comedy of a schoolteacher coping with his arranged marriage, was the first collaboration between the trio and the first fruit of Merchant Ivory Productions. Later, **Bombay Talkie** (1970) looked at the affair between a British writer and an Indian movie-star. It wasn't until his sixth film, **The Wild Party** in 1974, that Ivory tackled a period piece, which was in this case an adaptation of Joseph Moncure March's poem about 1920s' Hollywood. The first of his adaptations of literary classics was Henry James' 'The Europeans' in 1979. Since then, he has mostly stuck to novel adaptations, tackling Jean Rhys (**Quartet**, 1981), more James (**The Bostonians**, 1984; **The Golden Bowl**, 2000), E. M. Forster (**A Room with a View**, 1985; **Maurice**, 1987; **Howards End**, 1992). Other films include **Heat and Dust** (from Jhabvala's own novel, 1982), **Slaves of New York** (1989), **Mr & Mrs Bridge** (from books by Evan S. Connell, 1990), his masterful **The Remains of the Day** (from Kazuo Ishiguro's novel, 1993), **Jefferson in Paris** (1995) and **Surviving Picasso** (1996).

interview

I had been commissioned by The Asia Society of New York to make a documentary about Delhi, and travelled to India. There I became friendly with Satyajit Ray, and on a trip to Calcutta he invited me to go to the set of **Two Daughters**, (or **Three Daughters** as it was originally called; one of the stories was cut out by Ray's American distributor because it was too long). I remember getting up at absolutely the crack of dawn to be out there on set in the country. It was the last day of work on one of the stories, 'The Postmaster', and I just watched and watched. It was the first time I had ever seen a director at work. Even though I had gone to USC film school [University of Southern California], we had never visited a Hollywood film set in all the years I was there. I don't think I knew what a director did until I went on Ray's set and I saw him communicating all sorts of things to the actors in various kinds of ways, and muttering things to his cameraman. At that point, he had begun to operate his own camera, which is something his cameramen were not thrilled about, but they could hardly stop him. And I understand now why a director would want to operate his own camera if he could, especially for Ray, who couldn't do a lot of takes because Kodak film was so hard to get in India at the time. He would know at once whether he had got what he wanted out of his actors in terms of timing and composition in a way the cameraman could not.

And when I came to do my first feature, **The Householder**, two years later in Delhi with Ismail, we were able to hire his first cameraman, Subrata Mitra, and about 15 of his crew, including his first assistant. So in a sense, what they knew was what I learned during the nuts-and-bolts part of making a movie. I had never sat down and done a breakdown of a scene or a shot before then. It was like jumping into cold water, but I had to be able to do that.

I think **The Householder** naturally benefited from the fact that I was with Ray's long-time collaborators, and aesthetically there was further benefit, because I was looking at a scene through the eyes of his cameraman. When we came to editing the film, as we weren't happy with it – it was long and draggy and not cleverly edited – Ismail and I asked Ray if we could bring the film to show him, so we put ten reels of sound, ten reels of pictures and a lot of rushes in some big tin trunks and went on a train from Bombay to Calcutta. He liked the film and agreed to help us shape it, but on the condition that he do it freely with his editor, Dulal Dutta, and we not interfere. "Leave me alone for two or three days," he said. Anyway, he worked out a whole new scheme for the actual story and shortened it considerably, and gave it the flashback form it has today, within bookends. When we did **Shakespeare Wallah** later on, we again showed it to Ray, who suggested how we might tidy it up a bit, and he agreed to do the music.

I feel that I have never really found a better way to set my scenes than the way Ray taught me, or a way I *like* better, to put it another way. Somehow unconsciously and without a tremendous amount of analysis on my part, simply seeing his films over and over has worked on me in a way, so that, although I'm dealing with different kinds of subject matter and in countries thousands of miles away from India, I feel his influence very strongly. Some years after I've finished a movie and I'm looking at it, I realise that I wouldn't have done it that way if it had not been for Ray's lingering influence.

I never talked to Ray about this, but I feel he must have had similar ideas about working – in that I feel that if you hire good actors, then they are artists through and through, and what they give you is the gift of their talent. A director is crazy not to recognise this and accept it. There are times of course when actors get on the wrong track and you have to guide them back. But I've always felt that actors are very deep and not wide – that they go into the depths of their own character to create this new character for you. And on the other hand, directors are wide but not deep, because a director has to deal with hundreds of things going on horizontally and he must deal with all of those things confidently, but he may not be able to deal with them in the depth that he would like. He hasn't got the time; he has to spread himself more thinly than the actors do. But that makes for a good balance, and it carries over into his working relationship with his other collaborators. A director, for example, can't know every tiny nuance of every single take, whereas the editor has an incredible memory for that and knows exactly where any shot goes out of focus or where an actor stumbles on a line. It's impossible for a director to know all that – anyway, I can't. I'm famous for my sets and

1

```
                                        80
                    STEVENS
    Racy?

                    MISS KENTON
    Are you reading a racy book?

                    STEVENS
    You don't think "racy" books are to be
    found on his lordship's shelves, do you?

                    MISS KENTON
    How would I know?  What is it?  Let me
    see it.  Let me see your book.

                    STEVENS
    Miss Kenton, please leave me alone.

    She smiles and moves closer to him.  He wards her off.

                    MISS KENTON
    Why won't you show me your book?

                    STEVENS
    This is my private time.  You are
    invading it.

                    MISS KENTON
    Oh, is that so?  I am invading your
    private time, am I?

    She moves closer.

        What's in that book?  Come on.  Let me
        see.  Or are you protecting me?  Is
        that what you're doing?  Would I be
        shocked?  Would it ruin my character?

    They both stand quite still.

        Let me see it.

    She gently begins to take the book from him, lifting his
    fingers one at a time from the book.  This takes place
    in silence, their bodies very close.

    She opens the book and flicks through it.

                    MISS KENTON
    Oh dear, it's not scandalous at all.
    It's just a sentimental old love story.

    They look at each other.
```

2

(1–6) **The Remains of the Day**: (4) One of Ivory's most celebrated scenes is the tense exchange between Mr Stephens (Anthony Hopkins) and Miss Kenton (Emma Thompson) in **The Remains of the Day**, when Miss Kenton tries to discover the nature of the book Stephens is reading. "Here is a man who's given himself up to his work and his employer's crackpot ideas, and here is a woman who tries to get close to him, to get past all that. Such a situation could only exist in a great house in England between a butler and a housekeeper, a situation with such dynamics of repression and affection. We rehearsed it in several different ways, although the result was pretty much the same and we had several ways of going in the editing. I knew that what we were doing was something very very good." As Ivory points out, he and the actors didn't deviate from the script for the scene (2) at all, once in front of the cameras. (1, 6) Ivory shooting on location with Anthony Hopkins and Ismail Merchant, and on set.

3

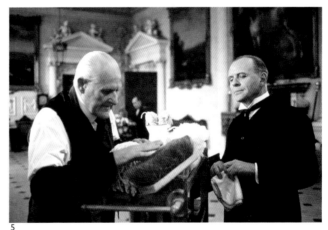

4

145

james ivory

5

6

1

2

3

(1–3) Ivory's admiration for actors is clear when he talks about Joanne Woodward and Paul Newman in **Mr & Mrs Bridge**. "I thought the scene when Mr Bridge comes home and finds Mrs Bridge decorating the Christmas tree, after their friend Grace has killed herself, and she breaks down and cries out, 'she was my friend', was extraordinary. Or when Austin Pendleton comes in out of the snow to talk to Mrs Bridge and try to sell her the magazine subscriptions. Often you feel it when you're shooting that some wonderful things are being captured." (2–3) Ivory's notes on the scene where a tornado hits the country club.

costumes, but I don't begin to know how the designers come up with these things. I just get very good people to do them, and I let them do what they know best.

So I think I work with actors in the same way that Ray did: I have a tremendous amount of respect for them. It's hard for me to understand how some directors can push actors around and humiliate them – and I hear terrible things from actors about the most famous directors. I couldn't work in that way. I don't tend to shove people around or yell and scream anyway. There was a famous actor we worked with once who had too long fingernails, and I felt that the character he was playing wouldn't have such long nails. It was very hard for me to bring it up without saying "goddamn it, cut your nails", so I didn't say anything, and there he is in the film with long nails. Sometimes you can't get your own way because you will offend the actor and disrupt something else that they are doing, which is not worth it. It's better to have long nails and wonderful performances. A director sees a million things. A leading lady might be conscious that one angle is better than another, yet you see that the angle she thinks is bad is really her best angle and you have to work to manouevre her in such a way or into such a position that the camera will take advantage of the better angle which they hate. Often you have to work secretly with the cameraman to do something or other. There's a lot of secrecy that goes on all through the making of a movie to enable the director to get his way.

When I'm casting, I've learned to be more open-minded than I used to be. There have been casting mistakes in some of our movies – more in the earlier ones – and one has to be more receptive to suggestions from agents and one's friends about actors. What I'm always looking for – and this is true even when casting a well-known star – is a kind of individual distinction. I don't like them to be conventional in appearance or personality; I want there to be some additional thing that brings some extra life. When we're casting new, young actors, we rarely choose some pretty girl or good-looking guy. Leelee Sobieski [in **A Soldier's Daughter Never Cries**], for example, was only 14 when we cast her, but she doesn't look like your average girl. She's about seven feet tall and has a marked aquiline nose, which gives her face a kind of strength and character that an ordinary pretty girl wouldn't have.

We always intended to have long dialogue scenes in our films. Earlier on when we worked with Subrata Mitra, we would very often do a whole scene in one shot, a combination of tracking and zooming and so forth and we'd get all the dialogue in one shot. Later on I did less of that. Such shots were difficult to edit. With conventional scenes from one viewpoint, such as the actors acting Shakespeare in **Shakespeare Wallah**, we have always worked in the classical way, which is to light for the long shots and then, on a particular angle, go in closer and closer to the tighter shots, and then reverse and light the other way and again get closer and closer. That's pretty traditional, and Ray's crew had been trained to do that. We still stick to that way of shooting. In India, it was very hard sometimes to do elaborate tracking shots because they don't have good dollies, and the floors were often uneven so it was difficult to lay rail – or sometimes we didn't have enough rail. Nevertheless in **Bombay Talkie**, we made very good use of long travelling shots in that film, which Mitra and I worked out carefully and which really paid off.

There are all kinds of ways of breaking a scene down. If it's a straightforward dialogue scene with people moving around a

1

2

3

Cinematographer Tony Pierce-Roberts has shot seven of Ivory's films, including **A Room with a View** (5–6) and **Howards End** (1–3). "I started off with Subrata Mitra, who was sometimes a very difficult man, but who gave me invaluable training as to what cameramen want and don't want. I know the kinds of things that throw them, the kind of shooting situations which are bad for them and which are going to put them in a bad temper. Tony is very easy to work with – he's not a temperamental man, although he's full of temper. He knows what I think at certain times, and we talk in a general way before we make the film. With **Howards End**, for example, I had done a number of period films by then and felt that we couldn't repeat what we had already done, so Tony decided to shoot in Super 35, because when we printed we could have 70mm prints. We also used a new, punchier kind of Kodak stock that he'd found that gave it a brasher look. Or on **The Golden Bowl**, which was the first film we shot anamorphic, I wanted the lavish backgrounds to be less well-defined and have a soft, painterly look. I didn't want the background to take away from what was going on. The film is about millionaires, living in houses full of art treasures, but I didn't want that to overwhelm the drama." (3) Ivory with lead Emma Thompson.

4

5

(5–6) Ivory and Pierce-Roberts were aiming for a sunny, bright and springlike feel for **A Room with a View**. Ivory has also worked with prolific cinematographer Pierre Lhomme, on **Maurice**, **Quartet** and **Jefferson in Paris**. (4) Ivory (centre) with his long-time partners – writer Ruth Prawer Jhabvala (left) and Ismail Merchant (right).

6

room and alighting here and there and sitting and standing, it's all rehearsed before we start and we don't need these tracking shots. The scene is broken down into shots so we know what we're going to do, and we follow that plan. But sometimes the scene is covered in one long master-shot, which we then break into with closer shots for emphasis.

I'm considered to be a perfectionist, but I also don't believe in doing too many takes because the actors hate it, and chances are they've given their best already and from then on, they get worse and worse.

Because of the kind of money we have, it's very rare to be able to bring the actors together before a shoot begins for rehearsal. Emma Thompson literally arrived on **The Remains of the Day** the day before we began shooting because she had another film going. There are only two films where we've had proper rehearsals – **Autobiography of a Princess**, which was very short, but we were able to plan rehearsals with James Mason and Madhur Jaffrey which really paid off; and **Mr & Mrs Bridge**, where we were able to have a proper two-week rehearsal period because we were all in New York. Also, Paul Newman and Joanne Woodward wanted very much to get to know the actors playing their kids. We even blocked some of the scenes, although I remember that when we got to Kansas City to shoot, I threw them all out of the window because they didn't apply to where we were shooting. I'm sure the rehearsals helped the wonderful performances in that film. Usually we do read-throughs beforehand, and when we're going to shoot we rehearse thoroughly on the day. For example, when we shot the scene where Maggie tells the Prince about her dream in **The Golden Bowl**, it was Kate Beckinsale's second day of work.

But she felt confident and so we went into the room and rehearsed it several ways. She ended up sitting on that couch at the foot of the bed with him down on his knees in front of her. I think there's a logic to any scene which is set in an existing room with furniture in it and doors and windows. You have to manage something within that – it's not like a set where you can take a whole wall out or shoot from above. It's therefore slightly inflexible, but the actors always manage it. You just rehearse it over and over until they're happy that they've moved about in a way that seems logical. It's an actor's logic. I have very good cameramen who, if the actors want to do their lines under a bed, will find a way to shoot it. Anyway, after we've organised a scene and the actors are satisfied, they then go into make-up and costume and the lighting is arranged, and we shoot it when they reappear.

Ruth and I go on working on the script right the way through shooting. She rarely comes on set because she doesn't like to; she always feels she's going to get in the way. But we keep in close touch over the phone and fax or by letters sometimes, and she watches the rushes all the time. She often picks up on things which feel repetitive and rewrites scenes we haven't shot accordingly, or if I tell her that someone is not working out as well as we thought, she will simplify speeches – or vice versa; if someone turns out to be brilliant, she will pump up their part. Sometimes she'll think we don't need a scene and will tell me to look at it again carefully because it could be a waste of film. That happened in **The Golden Bowl** with the Prince, Maggie and the little boy asleep in the bed at the end – that was originally two scenes.

When I'm doing films based on very well-known novels, I am not keen on actors improvising all over the place, nor am I

(1–4) Ivory and Merchant shot two different versions of their first film **The Householder**, one in English and one in Hindi (the latter was to be released only in India). Using bilingual actors, they literally shot both at the same time, "doing five takes on a shot in Hindi and five in English. If the weight of a scene was on an actor who was better in Hindi than English, we would do that one first so that he would understand what had to be done, and then we would do the English one. You'd think that it would be a slow way of working, but actually it didn't take any longer than normal." It was the editing that took longer – cutting and then mixing two complete versions. (1) Ivory with cameraman Subrata Mitra, on loan from Ivory's mentor Satyajit Ray.

(1–4) Ivory and Ruth Jhabvala decided to aim for long scenes of dialogue in **The Golden Bowl**, which would build to a conclusion more powerfully than several short scenes. The scene in which the golden bowl itself is smashed lasts seven minutes (5). "It pays off," says Ivory.

keen on them taking the novel and suggesting we re-insert scenes from it. When we were making **The Europeans**, everybody had a paperback copy of the book and was wandering around reading it all the time. Ruth knows exactly what she's doing; she's thought it out 500 times, and on the whole there is no need not to speak lines as written. Most actors tend to respect that, although any director's a fool if someone comes along with a better idea for a line and he doesn't accept it. Ruth also gets involved in the editing room. I change the film enormously in the editing. The first full screening is usually a vast, shapeless monster, and we do a lot between then and the final cut. There's stuff in the movie which isn't first class, but sometimes you are forced to keep such scenes in because they help the story. You must find a cut to present them in the best possible way. We don't reshoot. It's never as good as what we did the first time, even when it was done badly. We do add scenes sometimes, like the scene in **The Golden Bowl** where Maggie is reading the letter in the courtyard, which strengthens a particular strand of the story, and which was shot months later.

Critics of course only respond depending on whether we are in a fashionable or unfashionable phase in our career and reputations. We have been in and out of favour numerous times the whole 40 years we've been working. It all just washes away finally. We just carry on making films, and what we do is often the only thing like it out there. I do feel that we're a little bit like aliens in a way – from outer space.

Ivory and cameraman Subrata Mitra imported an Elemac dolly to shoot **Bombay Talkie**. "It took forever to set up that opening scene shot because all our equipment was rather primitive. The film begins with a dirty rag like a curtain over the frame, which is pulled back to reveal Ismail Merchant's face, as he and the Lucia Lane character come on the set as they are shooting the typewriter sequence. So we follow them and we go back a little more and a little bit more and a little bit more, and finally we come to the end of the track to reveal this giant red typewriter with all these girls dancing on the keys."

Bernardo Bertolucci's career as a director started when he was just 20. Having worked as assistant director to Pier Paolo Pasolini on his first feature **Accattone**, he made his co-writing and directing debut aged 21 with a Pasolini story called **The Grim Reaper (La Commare Secca)** in 1962, followed by the acclaimed **Before the Revolution (Prima della Rivoluzione)** in 1964. He came into his own with the

bernardo bertolucci

accomplished TV reinterpretation of Jorge Luis Borges' story 'The Spider's Stratagem' ('La Strategia del Ragno') (1970) and his astoundingly confident film of Alberto Moravia's 'The Conformist' ('Il Conformista') (1969). Both dealt with the politics of society, family and sexuality, recurring issues in all his films. His renown as a leading light in Italian cinema and a top international talent was sealed with his notorious **Last Tango in Paris** in 1972. In his following films, working in English, using American actors and his stalwart cinematographer Vittorio Storaro, Bertolucci fashioned a series of pictures with intimate themes set against a grand historical canvas: **1900** (1976) was a vast social drama spanning the class struggle in Italy in the first half of the 20th century; **The Last Emperor** (1987) a portrait of the fall of the Chinese empire to Communism; **The Sheltering Sky** (1990), a misunderstood adaptation of Paul Bowles' novel set in the '40s; and **Little Buddha** (1993), about the modern-day search for the reincarnation of Buddha and the ancient story of Prince Siddhartha. By 1995, he was back making films in Italy – **Stealing Beauty** and **Besieged** (1998).

Because my father was a poet, in some ways I too was condemned to be one, and as soon as I started to read and write, the first things I wrote were poems. Then at the age of 16 a relative gave me a 16mm camera, which is a great chance for the initiation for a 16-year-old director. It was a great liberation to be able to make my first film, a ten-minute movie called **La Teleferica**, because poetry was becoming a bit tight for me. I was just becoming an imitator of my father in poetry. Now cinema belonged to me. When I was 18 or 19, I was sent to Paris and I discovered the Cinémathèque Francaise. It was the year **A Bout de Souffle** came out and I went to see it four or five times. I was crazy about films and very early on, I became absorbed by the close-ups, wide shots or camera movements in them. Somebody next to me might have been crying because a couple was separating in the film; I was crying because the camera movement was so sublime.

When I was back in Rome, I started university, and one day Pier Paolo Pasolini knocked on the door of the house where my family was living. We were living on the fifth floor, he was

1

2

(1–4) **Last Tango in Paris** was made, "in a very innocent way. I didn't know it was so daring. I certainly didn't know I would have been condemned to two months in prison in Italy. The Catholic Church didn't like it but society at large loved it. When you adjust the inflation, it still holds the record for the biggest Italian hit in Italy. I send faxes to my friend Roberto Benigni telling him that **Life is Beautiful** may be number one now but **Last Tango** still holds the real record. And it made all its money in three months, because then it was banned." (1) Bertolucci with lead Maria Schneider.

3

directing

4

living on the first floor, and he said to me, "you are always talking about movies. I'm going to make a movie soon, I want you to be my assistant director". I told him I'd never done anything like that, and he said neither had he directed a film. Pasolini was an incredibly sophisticated writer, essayist, linguist, critic, poet and novelist, but he was still quite distant from cinema at this point. He had worked a bit with Fellini and Bolognini, but had no experience of the literal side of film-making and needed to understand what cinema meant. That meant that I assisted Pasolini in inventing cinema. It was a fantastic experience. It was like being next to Griffith as he invented cinema. Pasolini was always thinking that visually he wanted to be close to the primitive painting of Tuscany in the 14th and 15th centuries. I remember him telling me, when we were in a slum shooting a scene from **Accattone**, to look at how beautiful the grass was and doesn't it look like the background, or *sfondo*, of these primitive paintings. When he decided to do a dolly shot, it felt like we were doing the first dolly movement in cinema. It was the emotion of discovery.

When I was making my first film, **The Grim Reaper**, I consciously wanted a different style than Pasolini, so I avoided still shots for the most part and kept the camera moving all the time. Pasolini was frontal in a Byzantine style, whereas my camera was always moving around the characters. Whereas the camera was almost invisible in his films, in mine it became an additional character. It was anything but discreet and has a kind of sensual, loving relationship with the characters, sometimes favouring one over the other. That determined my language of cinema. **Before the Revolution** came second, a kind of autobiography, the opposite of **The Grim Reaper**.

Technically I had no knowledge, but I think I had a vision, and that's why I always tell young people who want to be directors to go and see as many movies as they can. My technical knowledge was based on the fact that I liked a shot which Godard or some other director had done. I knew exactly what I wanted but didn't technically know how, so I started to materialise my own vision. It was harder to be accepted on the set of **The Grim Reaper** because I was only 21 and the youngest of the group. I was attempting all these elaborate shots but had never done them before, so it was like jumping into the sea and learning how to swim at the same time. Because I was coming from poetry, I thought cinema was just an extension of that at first. That the camera was like another pen to write with. Later I understood that I was completely wrong, and that a movie is a collaborative work in which the director is the link. There has to be somebody like the director to trigger a creative excitement and libido in everyone. Also, when I shot the final scene of **1900** in which the landowner is on trial and the peasants want to lynch him, I used real people from the local farms to play the parts actually taken in real life by their parents at the Liberation in 1945. It was then that I realised that film is actually incredibly sensitive – more sensitive than its description as 500 ASA or 1,000 ASA. Film can absorb the feelings of the people for whom the drama was a reality; likewise the director can act as a bridge between the actors and the story. The older I get, the more I believe that film is a collective work.

I remember when I went to see Jean Renoir in L.A. in 1974. "You always have to leave a door open," he said, "because you never know when somebody will want to come in." That is exactly the philosophy I have embraced since I started. There is something which happens which is more important than the

(1–7) **1900**: "Some actors have opposite styles," says Bertolucci in reference to his two leads in **1900** – Robert De Niro (1) and Gérard Depardieu (2), both pictured with the director. "They were like two animals studying each other. Bob really is a method actor, and Burt Lancaster was to some extent, while Sterling Hayden and Gérard weren't, which was strange because Bob and Burt played landowners and Sterling and Gérard were farmers. I had to talk to Bob about every scene, which was an effort and removed a certain naturalness and innocence from the film. The only method for Gérard was to push him into the shot and bang... he was acting."

1900: Bertolucci spent a stunning 46 weeks shooting **1900**, his 1976 "intimate epic", which spanned the years 1900–45 in the lives of two men from the Po Valley. The 240-minute film contained one extraordinary 40-minute sequence in which De Niro's character Alfredo marries Ada, played by Dominique Sanda (4). In the revelry that follows, fascist supporter Attila, played by Donald Sutherland, (6, right) rapes and murders a child. "It was like a movie within the movie. I felt it was inspired by **La Règle du Jeu** because of the ballet, and there was that scene which my wife, who was my assistant, thought was terrible and I shouldn't have shot. At the time, I thought that fascists were terrible and did terrible things, so everything was black and white. Now I feel it's terrible to watch. I remember closing my eyes when the scene played, and I still close my eyes because I know that scene is coming."

1900: Produced by Alberto Grimaldi, the film ran over budget fairly early on in its shooting schedule. "We stayed for so long in the Po Valley that the crew became very attached to it. One day I just set a deadline and said that we were going to finish the movie next Saturday. Many people in the crew didn't talk to me after that."

6

7

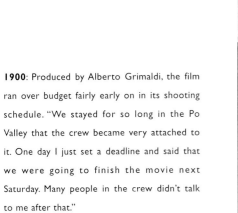

screenplay, and that is what an actor or actress can bring to the story from their own experience. The characters on the page feel literary but the actors give them flesh and blood, and with that comes their own experiences, memories, pain and baggage. This adds a whole new dimension and is often more interesting than the story. In fact when you finish the screenplay, it is just the beginning really. It's just a blueprint for what you can do. That means, of course, that the casting is very important, especially when I choose someone over somebody else. It's often based on strong intuition, as I have to feel really fascinated by the personalities of the people who will be in front of the camera for weeks and weeks, and that they have enough secrets and experience for me to discover.

When I'm working on the screenplay, I try to focus on what the literary experience of the story will be. In fact if you look at Italian cinema, one of the problems sometimes in movies, even masterpieces, is the dialogue. Antonioni's, and Fellini's movies, show extraordinary visual invention, but in some of the movies the words spoken are unbearable, unacceptable. The reason behind the fact I prefer to shoot in English is that it is a language much closer to cinema than Italian. If I wrote a screenplay in English, it would be 110 pages, but if I ask to translate it, it would come out at 140 pages. The same thing made into more words. I discovered that when I shot with Marlon Brando, because he could say the same thing with few words, even though we had to communicate in French because my English was so poor. The dialogue was so dry and every word so essential. Italian is good for poetry and opera but not for film-making.

I used to think that directors should write their own films, but now I don't. When I started, I was so nervous that I had to be in control of everything. In secret you think you are shit, that maybe you won't be able to do the next shot or the one after that. The more confident I became, the more I began to accept working with other people. You see that someone can bring more ideas and can provoke discussion. I saw **Before the Revolution** at Cannes in 2000 for the first time in 36 years and was amazed how sure we were of our ideas. I was politically extreme, convinced that I was right and everybody else was wrong – the way people walked through society was very different. For a long time now though, I've been living in great doubts.

The cinema of the '60s was a seminal time in the history of cinema, like the late '20s, when cinema started to talk, or the late '30s when colour came in. It was when cinema started to think: "Qu'est-ce que c'est, le cinema?" In the '60s we were so obsessed with what cinema is and by style and language, and of course our movies were very elliptical, very hermetic and very difficult for audiences. We were pushing away audiences and the films weren't making money, so we found it harder to raise money, therefore it was also very masochistic. At the end of the '60s, I felt at a dead end. I felt our movies were almost monologues about ourselves to ourselves. I wanted to reach people and have a dialogue. My friends, I think, felt that I was selling my soul to the market, the devil's market, but for me everything happened very naturally because I was asked by Italian TV channel RAI to do **The Spider's Stratagem**, and that was naturally for a large audience because it was made for TV. By the time I made **The Conformist**, I actually found great pleasure in making a movie, which was strange to me because pleasure was something associated with being right-wing. I don't think about the audience when I'm making a movie because it's a

1

2

(1–3) **The Conformist**: When he was cutting **The Spider's Stratagem**, Bertolucci was asked to direct a film of 'The Conformist', from the Alberto Moravia novel, so he postponed completion of the former, wrote the screenplay to the latter in just a month, and shot it. Cinematographer on both films was Vittorio Storaro. Together with production designer Fernando Scarfiotti, Bertolucci and Storaro rediscovered Italian fascist architecture of the '30s, which still held associations with fascist atrocities, and used it to great effect in the film – from the EUR outside Rome to Mussolini's ready-built city of Sabaudia, designed by the architect Adalberto Libera. "People who lived in that period asked me how I could create such an accurate portrait of fascism at the age of 28, not just in costume and set design but also in mood, but for me it was inspired completely by the American and French movies of those years directed by Raoul Walsh, Jean Renoir and all the others."

3

directing

1

2

(1) Bertolucci on location in the Forbidden City for **The Last Emperor** and in the North African desert for **The Sheltering Sky** (2). Bertolucci's trilogy of non-Italian epics – **The Last Emperor**, **The Sheltering Sky** and **Little Buddha** – were seen by many as incongruous with his earlier work. "I enjoy changing. Somebody called **The Last Emperor** my Hollywood film, but I don't see it as that, I think it's more like an Italian opera, a 'Turandot', certainly much more European than American. It's the loneliest story because Pu Yi is always a prisoner, of his family and of himself. I like it when the epics have a sense of intimacy."

completely fake concept. Nobody knows how an audience will react, and it's an illusion if you do something because you think the audience will like it.

I try to be as close as possible to my actors and as fascinated with them as I can. I want my camera to be in love with them. All the films are love stories with the actors over the eight, ten or 15 weeks of shooting. When you see a good performance, a rich character, that's what makes the movie worthwhile for me. I never do rehearsals with actors before the shoot. We do everything on set. I don't like to talk about the scene with actors away from the set because it's too relaxed away off-set. On the set you have the objects and the costumes which put the actors into the mood. I respect people who do rehearsals before a shoot, but it's against my nature. Cinema came from theatre, where you do a lot of rehearsals, but cinema is different from theatre. I would hate to capture something on film which blossomed the week before during rehearsals. The same magic can't then be reinvented in front of the camera.

The camera is somebody, the camera is the reason why the two characters in **Last Tango in Paris** say all those silly things to each other. They need the camera and the camera needs them, so there is a basic relationship there. I know nothing technically. I can take a Polaroid shot but there's not much skill in that. So while I'm very technical when I prepare the shots with my viewfinder, the camera then has to do exactly what I want. I know about lenses and movements, but I'm not good at lighting. When Vittorio Storaro and I first worked together on **The Spider's Stratagem**, I couldn't describe what I wanted very clearly so I showed him paintings. One was a famous one, [René Magritte's] 'L'Empire des Lumières' – 'Empire of Lights' – with a house, trees and a

streetlamp, but it's daytime in the sky, and then you move down to the earth, and then it's night. There's this nighttime blue, and we used this blue throughout the movie. I am unable to paint and Vittorio was like my hand painting with his camera. He did the light and the colours, although the colours are as much about production design and costume design. The camera, however, is my toy and so I speak a lot to the camera operator to get exactly the shot I want.

In **1900**, there are four distinct colour schemes to go with the seasons. The childhood is very solemn, impressionistic, and it becomes cooler and cooler for the winter when fascism comes in, and then lighter in spring for the Liberation. When we were shooting **The Last Emperor**, I told Vittorio the story of this man who goes from darkness to light ideologically and goes from being an emperor in prison to a free man. So he wrote in his essays that the colour in the first part should be very dark and de-coloured and then the colour would arrive with the cultural revolution, and so on. But I said, no, Vittorio, the colour has to be in the childhood. He objected, saying that I had told him the opposite. And I said, yes, it's true, but visually we have to go this way. So the first part is very colourful and brilliant and free of everything.

I enjoy not doing the same thing. I like intimate movies like **Last Tango in Paris** or **Besieged** to have an epic flavour. In the same way, I like male actors to have something feminine about them and actresses to have something masculine.

My father died this year and I don't know what I will do now. I think my cinema will change. Maybe I won't do any more films, you never know. I'm curious to know what will happen, but I really don't know.

Milos Forman is that rare breed of film-maker, who has had a major impact on both European and Hollywood cinema. His early films in Communist Czechoslovakia mocked the system under which he lived and led the extraordinary Czech New Wave movement of the '60s. On moving to the US in 1969, it was only five years before he created arguably the defining film of the '70s – **One Flew Over the Cuckoo's Nest**.

milos forman

Born in 1932, he attended FAMU (Film Academy of the Arts) in Prague, where he studied screenwriting. He made his feature-directing debut in 1963 with **Black Peter (Cerny Petr)**, following it with **The Loves of a Blonde (Lásky Jedné Plavovlásky)** in 1965, and the controversial allegory **The Firemen's Ball (Horí, má Panenko**, 1967). Moving to New York in 1969, Forman made his first US film **Taking Off** in 1971, winning him a jury prize at Cannes. He followed it four years later with **Cuckoo's Nest**, which was a huge box-office hit as well as making a clean sweep at that year's Academy Awards. His subsequent films – mostly adaptations of hit novels or stage shows – are united by their brilliant storytelling and bravura performances as well as a distinctly anti-establishment tone, and in **Hair** (1979), **Ragtime** (1981), **The People vs. Larry Flynt** (1996) and **Man on the Moon** (1999), a refreshingly objective view of America – both its greatnesses and its follies. He shot two films in Europe – the much-loved **Amadeus** (1984) and **Valmont** (1988), his excellent and overlooked film of 'Les Liaisons Dangereuses', the novel by Pierre Choderlos de Laclos.

When I was growing up, I was more fascinated by theatre than film because it was so alive in front of my eyes, so I originally applied to study theatre at the drama school in Prague but was not accepted. The next best thing was the film school and, happily for me, because otherwise I would have had to do military service, I was accepted. For the four years at film school, I saw a lot of films which other people in Communist countries were not allowed to see, and in those four years I developed a passion for the movies. What mainly pushed my buttons was the discovery of American silent comedy – Chaplin, Keaton, Laurel and Hardy, Harold Lloyd, Ben Turpin. They provoked some kind of ambition in me. Also it was the time of Italian neo-realism and, because those films were critical of capitalist society, we saw them all. Strangely enough, they had exactly the opposite effect on us that the idealogues wanted. Instead of showing us how awful and tragic capitalism was, these films were symbols of freedom. On the one hand, the idealogues were telling us about the oppression of free art in Western society, and yet on the other, these artists criticising society were making such wonderful

1

2

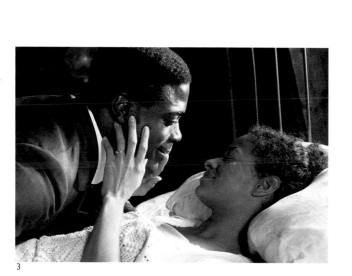

3

4

5

7

8

9

(1–9) **Ragtime**: In adapting 'Ragtime', E. L. Doctorow's epic novel of 1906 America to the screen, Forman abandoned many of the historical figures in the book in favour of a focus on one fictional character in particular – black pianist Coalhouse Walker, played by Howard Rollins Jr. Central to Forman's vision is the scene where firemen fill Walker's car with horse excrement, an action which drives him to become militant in his quest for justice. "Suddenly he is confronted with the choice to either accept the humiliation and walk away or ask justice of these people and therefore get into trouble. Of course this was a moment which reminded me of my life in Czechoslovakia, where you were confronted with this kind of dilemma every day. For me that is the nucleus of the film, and the other parts of the book about [Harry] Houdini and [Pierpoint] Morgan and [Henry] Ford didn't contribute to that conflict and that drama." Ironically, the sequences in which Emma Goldman [the famous Russo-American anarchist] appeared were cut out of the film on the recommendation of producer Dino De Laurentiis and Paramount Pictures, in an effort to cut down the running time. Forman is looking to restore the original footage to the DVD version of the film, although the negative was destroyed and only a black-and-white duplicate remains. Many of the exterior crowd scenes of New York were shot on sets at London's Shepperton Studios (2). "If you have a good set designer and you understand each other, he will give you enough space and angles. As a matter of fact, in some ways it's easier to shoot in the studios because you don't have any distractions." Among the rich ensemble cast were Brad Dourif (Younger Brother), Elizabeth McGovern (Evelyn Nesbit) and Mandy Patinkin (Tateh) pictured with Forman (1), Debbie Allen (Sarah), with Rollins (3), Kenneth McMillan (the racist fire chief Willie Conklin) (4) and Robert Joy (Harry K. Thaw, here seen shooting legendary architect Stanford White, as played by Norman Mailer) (6).

1

2

(1–3) Forman shot the **The Firemen's Ball** in the same hall, in the same small town, where he and co-writers Ivan Passer and Jaroslav Papousek had attended the firemen's ball which inspired them. The local firemen they befriended played the roles of the firemen in the film. "There wasn't a single trained actor in that film. The local townspeople also played the crowds in the film, and shooting would start when they finished their factory shifts at two in the afternoon."

3

and powerful movies. We, on the other hand, who had conquered capitalism thought we should be free to talk about it totally freely, but were making pieces of shit. These kinds of dilemmas were instrumental to me when I was young.

My generation was so lucky because I started making films sometime after Kruschev denounced Stalinism and declared that young people should have more opportunities. Up to 1963, there were about four or five films being made a year in Czechoslovakia, all by the old-time party members, and after that, there was an explosion and we started to make our movies. Fortunately the films got recognition abroad and they let you travel with them to festivals, although often accompanied by a watchdog.

The Loves of a Blonde was fine because people considered the film a comedy. The directors who made serious dramas got into trouble, but comedies had a much easier time of it. **The Firemen's Ball** opened for about two weeks in the summer of 1968, but the moment the Russians invaded Czechoslovakia and re-established tough political control, the film was officially banned forever.

Of course **The Firemen's Ball** was a metaphor, but while we were making it, I had to pretend to be totally ignorant of that. It started when my two friends Ivan Passer and Jaroslav Papousek and I started to work on a screenplay about something totally different. It wasn't going well: we even left Prague and went to a small town in the mountains just to cut ourselves off from other distractions. One evening, for fun, we went to a firemen's ball in the small mountainous town, and the next morning we couldn't talk about anything else. It had the same absurdity as ends up in the film.

We developed a friendship with the local firemen and spent a lot of time playing cards, drinking beer and playing billiards with them. At this same time, Carlo Ponti (the Italian producer) offered to co-produce my next film because he was impressed by the success of **The Loves of a Blonde**. So the $85,000 he invested enabled us to buy an Elemac, which at that time was a very sophisticated dolly without which we wouldn't have been able to shoot the sequence of events at the ball. When you have a room full of dancers, you can't put rails in-between them, so we had to have this Elemac which has very movable little wheels, so that the cameraman is being pushed any way he wants and it still looks steady. At the time, French *cinéma vérité* was a big inspiration for us, but we wanted to be different. We wanted to use the method but hide it, so that it's not seen: to tell a real story, not just catching moments of life as they happen. And we didn't want the shaky hand-held feel of their camera images. Also Ponti's money allowed us to shoot the film on Eastman Kodak and not on Orvo, which was a bad East German stock.

I prefer shooting in sequence because I like the script to develop more branches and grow during shooting. I was aware that this film is not the story of one protagonist and that it's just a series of vignettes, which is demanding on an audience's attention. I didn't expect the film to be so short, but we had to get rid of a lot of things in the editing just to keep the pace going.

Later, during the so-called Prague Spring, things were loosening up politically so, after that, they signed a contract for me to make one film in the US, and I tried to make **Taking Off** in the same way as I had made my Czech films. When it was a flop, I simply didn't want to go back to Czechoslovakia a loser, so I asked them to extend my exit visa, which they denied, so I stayed in the US anyway. At this point, I realised that as a writer in the US, I couldn't function in the language which I grew up with, but the English language has never been and never will be a way of speaking my thoughts. And so I realised that I'd better turn to material which was written by English-speaking authors, which meant adaptations. After **Taking Off**, I made a conscious decision to do that, rather than trying to transplant the methods I had already used when in Czechoslovakia.

That's how I came to the Ken Kesey novel. There was already one version of the script by Larry Hauben, and I worked with him on a second version to incorporate the way I saw how the film should be made. After a couple of months working together, we hit a block, and asked another writer to come in with a fresh look. That's when Bo Goldman stepped in. Because I didn't know much about the language or the country, I suggested we [Hauben and Forman] go and work on the script right there in the mental institution in Salem, Oregon, where we were going to shoot. We slept in the nurses' quarters, and every day we spent a couple of hours just wandering around watching the therapy sessions and talking to the patients.

Whereas the book was told from the point of view of the schizophrenic Indian, complete with all his surreal hallucinations, I wanted it to be very real in order to get across the horror and absurdity of the situation. In literature, surreal imagery helps you understand the horror, but on film that would put it in an unreal setting.

I was aware that the cast for this film would have to be very carefully chosen because it's more or less an ensemble piece,

so I had to orchestrate it that everybody had distinctive physicalities. I also realised that the world of the mental institution is unknown to us, so that one man who comes from outside should be someone I should identify with. That of course made it a perfect starring vehicle for Jack Nicholson. **The Last Detail**, **The King of Marvin Gardens** and **Five Easy Pieces** hadn't been successful, and **Chinatown** hadn't come out yet, so he wasn't yet a big box-office draw, but for me he was a star and he was my first choice. But once I had him, I wanted everybody in the unknown world into which he enters to be unknown. So I hired a lot of new faces. I auditioned over a thousand people for all the parts. Of course now they are all well-known – Danny DeVito, Christopher Lloyd, Brad Dourif, Louise Fletcher. We had real patients from the Salem hospital in the film because the dean of the hospital thought it would be good therapy for them.

Whenever I finish a film, I always put everything that was shot together so that it runs over three hours. Then you can see where it starts to drag and what is redundant or repetitious, so you start chopping it down. What was very interesting on **Cuckoo's Nest** was that I finally got it to, say two hours and 21 minutes, and it was still too long, so I got mad and chopped it to the bone – to about two hours. But then a strange thing happened: it felt even longer. By cutting it to the bone, I cut a lot of little seemingly unimportant details which made these characters interesting and human, and which somehow sucked you into these people. So then I edited back about eight minutes, and suddenly it felt fine.

Turning **Hair** into a movie was a challenge because the play didn't have a story at all. When I met potential writers, I would ask them how they imagined a film version, and one

1

2

3

4

5

(1–5) Forman was originally asked to read 'One Flew Over the Cuckoo's Nest', with a view to directing it, by Kirk Douglas who had bought the film rights in 1966; Douglas had been in Prague on a goodwill tour of Communist countries. However, when he sent Forman the book, it was confiscated by censors at customs without Forman or Douglas' knowledge. Douglas failed to get a film off the ground at the time, but ten years later, when Saul Zaentz and Douglas' son Michael had taken over the project, they sent Forman the book, "when I was lying on my bed in the Chelsea Hotel in New York after **Taking Off** and I was reading all these stupid scripts." Through Michael Douglas, he met Kirk again and they deduced what had happened ten years earlier. "Bizarrely, ten years later it was sent to me by his son. I guess I was destined to do it."

1

directing

2

3

4

5

6

7

(1–7) To prepare for **Amadeus**, Forman invited the author of the hit play, Peter Shaffer, to his house in Connecticut to work on the screenplay and the score. They remained there for three months, venturing out to New York for only one weekend. "The main thing was to avoid photographing the play. To tell the story in a moving way, or at least not a static one. As for the music, we worked it all out beforehand — we spent an hour a day on it. I love to have the music beforehand, and if I don't have it, I put some temp music on because it helps you think and feel the atmosphere much quicker and more deeply."

after the other they came up with this psychedelic babble about the cosmic consciousness. One day this guy Michael Weller came in, and I asked him how the play should be made into a film. And he said, "I don't have a fucking clue". That was language I understood, so I hired him and together we worked out a script. Of course Gerome Ragni and James Rado, who wrote the play, hated it and offered to write their own script. But their version was not a film script at all, it was another version of the play, and that is too limiting.

My philosophy is that whatever I'm adapting was not written out of thin air. Peter Shaffer read all of Mozart's letters and biographies and then used all this material as a springboard for his vision on the stage. Ken Kesey was the same. He had worked as an orderly in a mental institution and used it as a springboard for his vision of the world. When you are making a film based on this literature or play, you have to ask for the same right. Even E. L. Doctorow was not happy with **Ragtime**, because he had his own vision of how the novel should be filmed. I guess it's very difficult for the original author of a piece of work that is successful in its own medium to change anything. Peter Shaffer was brilliant in this respect, but by the time we did **Amadeus** he'd learned it the hard way, because all his plays have been filmed badly. Even **Equus**, for which he himself wrote the screenplay, didn't work.

So suddenly on **Amadeus**, he was prepared to open himself, to step into the darkness: to destroy the structure of the play and build a new structure for the film. The first challenge was how to tell the story. In the play Salieri talks to the audience, which of course wouldn't work. We realised that it was very simple. In those days, if you tried to commit suicide, they didn't send you to a doctor, they sent you to a priest, who is there to console your soul and ask for your confession. The moment we discovered that, we knew we had the frame for the whole structure. Then we made it more interesting by making the priest a young man who hadn't heard of Salieri – which makes him even more crazy. That somebody in Vienna, where he was a superstar for so many years, wouldn't know his music. That would drive him mad.

Another differentiating factor was the use of music. The theatre can't use music, because you can't hear the words if you play the music. Film devours music and you can hear both the music and the words. So the music became much more important. You couldn't have done that dictation scene in **Amadeus** on stage. Composing is the hardest thing on film, I think. I think I could do just about everything else. I could write, act, photograph, edit, but I can't compose music. I can see in my head how an actor should say a line, but I don't hear how music should create a mood in a scene. I remember after I sent the long version of **Cuckoo's Nest** to Jack Nitzsche so that he could start work on it, I called Jack and asked him what kind of orchestra he needed. And on the day of the recording session, he arrived with a short, skinny old man with a huge suitcase, and in that suitcase were 50 or 60 glasses and he started to pour water in the glasses. The music is all glass harmonica. Then he added some drums, Indian flute and electric saw. I couldn't believe it, it was wonderful.

Of course, ultimately, you have to tell a good story. If you're trying to tell somebody a story and that person's attention starts to wander, that's not good. The aim is to tell the truth without being boring. That's why lies are so successful, because the truth can be pretty boring – because it's the truth.

picture credits

Stills in Introduction: p6 **Holy Smoke** (Jane Campion, 1999) photography by Gerald Jenkins, Miramax Films/Film Four and courtesy of The Ronald Grant Archive (also on p78); p8, left **Traffic** (Steven Soderbergh, 2000) photography by Bob Marshak, with thanks and acknowledgement to Initial Entertainment Group, Inc. (also on p73); p8, right **Crouching Tiger, Hidden Dragon** (Ang Lee, 2000), Columbia Tri-Star/Sony Pictures Classics and courtesy of *Screen International* (also on p90); p9, left **Natural Born Killers** (Oliver Stone, 1994) photography by Sidney Baldwin, Warner Bros./Regency Enterprises V. O. F./Canal + and courtesy of The Ronald Grant Archive (also on p99); p9, right **Land and Freedom** (Ken Loach, 1995), Working Title Films/Parallax Pictures/Diaphana/Canal + Espana and courtesy of *Screen International* (also on p110); p10, left **The End of Violence** (Wim Wenders, 1991), with thanks and acknowledgement to CIBY 2000/Road Movies Filmproduktion/Kintop Pictures (also on p127); p10, right **Blue Velvet** (David Lynch, 1986), De Laurentiis Entertainment Group and courtesy of The Ronald Grant Archive; p11, left **Last Tango in Paris** (Bernardo Bertolucci, 1972), United Artists/P. E. A./MGM/Productions Artistes Associés and courtesy of The Ronald Grant Archive (also on p156); p11, right **Amadeus** (Milos Forman, 1984), Orion and courtesy of The Ronald Grant Archive (also on p172).

Courtesy of The Ronald Grant Archive: p2 **Last Tango in Paris**, United Artists/ P. E. A./MGM/Productions Artistes Associés (also on p156); p24 **Rosemary's Baby**, Paramount Pictures; p25 portrait shot from **Frantic**, Warner Bros./Mount; p26 **Macbeth**, Playboy Productions (2–4); p27 **Macbeth**, Playboy Productions (12, 14); p28 **The Ninth Gate**, R. D. Productions (1–3); p31 **Chinatown**, Paramount Pictures (3, 4); p32 **Rosemary's Baby**, Paramount Pictures (1–3, 6); p34 **Kikujiro**, Bandai Visual/Tokyo FM/Nippon Herald/Office Kitano; p44 **Naked**, Thin Man Films/British Screen/Film Four/Fine Line Features, photography by Simon Mein; p51 **Naked**, First Independent/Thin Man Films/British Screen/Film Four (4); p54 **Breaking the Waves**, Guild Pathe Cinema/Zentropa Entertainments Aps + La Sept Cinema; p56 **Breaking the Waves**, Guild Pathe Cinema/Zentropa Entertainments Aps + La Sept Cinema (1–3); p62 **The Idiots**, Metro Tartan/Zentropa Entertainments Aps + La Sept Cinema (1–4); p68 **Poor Cow**, VIC Films/Fenchurch Films (2); p76 **The Portrait of a Lady**, Polygram Filmed Entertainment, photography by Grant Matthews; p78 **Holy Smoke**, Miramax Films/Film Four, photography by Gerald Jenkins (4); p79 **Holy Smoke**, Miramax Films/Film Four, photography by Gerald Jenkins (6, 7); p83 **The Portrait of a Lady**, Polygram Filmed Entertainment (2); p83 **The Portrait of a Lady**, Polygram Filmed Entertainment, photography by Jürgen Teller (3, 4); p84 **Sweetie**, Arena Film (1, 2); p84 **An Angel at My Table**, Nibiscus Films/N. Z. Film Commission/TV New Zealand/ABC (3, 4); p94 **Sense and Sensibility**, Columbia Tri-Star (3); p96 **Natural Born Killers**, Warner Bros./Regency Enterprises V. O. F., photography by Sidney Baldwin; p99 **Natural Born Killers**, Warner Bros./Regency Enterprises V. O. F., photography by Sidney Baldwin (1–3); p99 **Natural Born Killers**, Warner Bros./Regency Enterprises V. O. F./Canal +, photography by Sidney Baldwin (4, 5); p100 **Natural Born Killers**, Warner Bros./Regency Enterprises V. O. F./Canal +, photography by Sidney Baldwin (1–3); p102 **Nixon**, Entertainment Films/Cinergi Productions (1, 2, 4); p102 **Nixon**, Entertainment Films/Cinergi Productions, photography by Sidney Baldwin (3); p103 **Nixon**, Entertainment Films/Cinergi Productions, photography by Sidney Baldwin (12); p105 **U Turn**, Columbia Tri-Star (1–7); p106 **JFK**, Warner Bros./Regency Enterprises V. O. F./Canal + (1–5); p108 **Poor Cow**, VIC Films/Fenchurch Films; p110 **Land and Freedom**, Working Title Films/Parallax Pictures/Diaphana/Canal + Espana (1, 3); p112 **Ladybird Ladybird**, UIP/Parallax Pictures (4, 5); p115 **Poor Cow**, VIC Films/Fenchurch Films (3, 4); p116 **Kes**, Woodfall Film Productions/Kestrel Films (1–3); p127 **Until the End of the World**, Road Movies Filmproduktion/Argos Films/Mathrab/Village Roadshold Corporation (3); p128 **Paris, Texas**, Road Movies Filmproduktion/Argos Films/Channel Four (1–3); p130 **Blue Velvet**, De Laurentiis Entertainment Group; p132 **The Elephant Man**, Brooksfilms (2, 3); p134 **Dune**, Universal Pictures (1–3); p135 **Blue Velvet**, De Laurentiis Entertainment Group (4–9); p138 **Twin Peaks: Fire Walk with Me**, Guild Film Distribution/Propaganda Films/Lynch/Frost Productions (1, 2); p139 **Twin Peaks: Fire Walk with Me**, Guild Film Distribution/Propaganda Films/Lynch/Frost Productions (4, 5); p140 **The Straight Story**, Canal +/The Picture Factory/Film Four (4); p154 **The Conformist**, Mars Film Produzione/Marianne Productions/Maran Film; p155 portrait shot from **Last Tango in Paris**, United Artists/ P. E. A./MGM/Productions Artistes Associés; p156 **Last Tango in Paris**, United Artists/ P. E. A./MGM/Productions Artistes Associés (1–4); p158–9 **1900**, United Artists/ P. E. A./MGM/Productions Artistes Associés/Artemis Filmgesellschaft (1–7); p161 **The Conformist**, Mars Film Produzione/Marianne Productions/Maran Film (1–3); p162 **The Last Emperor**, Yanco Films/TAO Film/Recorded Picture Co./Screenframe/AAA/Soprofilms (1); p162 **The Sheltering Sky**, Warner Bros. (2); p164 **One Flew Over the Cuckoo's Nest**, United Artists/Fantasy Films; p165 portrait shot from **One Flew Over the Cuckoo's Nest**, United Artists/Fantasy Films; p166–7 **Ragtime**, Paramount Pictures (1–9); p168 **The Firemen's Ball**, Ceskoslovensky Film/Filmové Studio Barrandov/Carlo Ponti Cinematografica (1–3); p171 **One Flew Over the Cuckoo's Nest**, United Artists/Fantasy Films (1–5); p172 **Amadeus**, Orion (1–7).

Courtesy of The Kobal Collection: p12 **Kika**, El Deseo/CIBY 2000; p14 **All About My Mother**, El Deseo/RENN/France 2/PATHÉ (1); p17 **Kika**, El Deseo/CIBY 2000 (3, 4); p20 **Tie Me Up! Tie Me Down!**, El Deseo (3, 5); p21 **Live Flesh**, El Deseo/CIBY 2000, photography by Daniel Martinez (10).

Courtesy of Screen International: p90 **Crouching Tiger, Hidden Dragon**, Columbia Tri-Star/Sony Pictures Classics (1); p94 **Sense and Sensibility**, Columbia Tri-Star, photography by Clive Coote (2); p110 **Land and Freedom**, Working Title Films/Parallax Pictures/Diaphana/Canal + Espana (2, 4).

Visual material contributed by Pedro Almodóvar: p13 portrait shot © Teresa Isasi, with thanks and acknowledgement to El Deseo; p14–15 **All About My Mother** (2–9) © Teresa Isasi, with thanks and acknowledgement to El Deseo; p17 **Kika** (1, 2) © Jean Marie Leroy, with thanks and acknowledgement to El Deseo/CIBY 2000; p18 from **All About My Mother** (1) © Teresa Isasi, with thanks and acknowledgement to El Deseo; p18 **High Heels** (2–4) © Mimmo Cattarinich, with thanks and acknowledgement to El Deseo/CIBY 2000; p20 **Tie Me Up! Tie Me Down!** (1, 2, 4, 6) photography by Mimmo Cattarinich, with thanks and acknowledgement to El Deseo; p21 **Live Flesh** (7–9) photography by Daniel Martinez, with thanks and acknowledgement to El Deseo; p21 **The Flower of My Secret** (11–13) © Jean Marie Leroy, with thanks and acknowledgement to El Deseo/CIBY 2000; p22 from **Women on the Verge of a Nervous Breakdown** (1–20) designs by Juan Gatti, with thanks and acknowledgement to El Deseo/Lauren Films.

Visual material contributed by Roman Polanski: p26 **Macbeth** (1) photography by Annette Green, with thanks and acknowledgement to Playboy Productions; p26 **Macbeth** (5–8), with thanks and acknowledgement to Playboy Productions; p27 **Macbeth** (9–11, 13), with thanks and acknowledgement to Playboy Productions; p28 **The Ninth Gate** (4–7), with thanks and acknowledgement to R. D. Productions; p31 **Chinatown** (1, 2), with thanks and acknowledgement to Paramount Pictures; p32 **Rosemary's Baby** (4, 5), with thanks and acknowledgement to Paramount Pictures.

Visual material contributed by Takeshi Kitano: p35 portrait shot; p36 **Hana-bi** (1–5), with thanks and acknowledgement to Bandai Visual/Television Tokyo/Tokyo FM/Office Kitano; p38–9 **Brother** (1–12), with thanks and acknowledgement to Little Brother Inc.; p41 (1); p41 **Kikujiro** (2, 3), with thanks and acknowledgement to Bandai Visual/Tokyo FM/Nippon Herald/Office Kitano; p42 **Kikujiro** (1), with thanks and acknowledgement to Bandai Visual/Tokyo FM/Nippon Herald/Office Kitano; p42 **A Scene at the Sea** (2, 3), with thanks and acknowledgement to Office Kitano/Totsu; p42 **Brother** (4), with thanks and acknowledgement to Little Brother Inc.

Visual material contributed by Mike Leigh: p45 portrait shot; p46 **Secrets & Lies** (1–3), with thanks and acknowledgement to Thin Man Films/CIBY 2000; p46 **Secrets & Lies** (4, 5) photography by Simon Mein, with thanks and acknowledgement to Thin Man Films/CIBY 2000; p47 **Secrets & Lies** (6–8) photography by Simon Mein, with thanks and acknowledgement to Thin Man Films/CIBY 2000; p48 (1); p48 **Topsy-Turvy** (2–6) photography by Simon Mein, with thanks and acknowledgement to Thin Man Films/Untitled 98 Ltd. ©; p51 **Naked** (1–3) photography by Simon Mein, with thanks and acknowledgement to Thin Man Films/British Screen/Film Four; p52 **Career Girls** (1–3) photography by Joss Barratt, with thanks and acknowledgement to Thin Man Films/Film Four; p52 **Secrets & Lies** (4) photography by Simon Mein, with thanks and acknowledgement to Thin Man Films/CIBY 2000.

Visual material contributed by Lars von Trier: p55 portrait shot; p56 **Breaking the Waves** (4, 5), with thanks and acknowledgement to Zentropa Entertainments Aps + La Sept Cinema; p58–9 **Dancer in the Dark** (1–4), with thanks and acknowledgement to Zentropa Entertainments Aps + La Sept Cinema/France 3 Cinema/Arte France Cinema/Trust Film Svenska/Liberator Productions/Dain Unlimited; p61 **The Element of Crime** (1–3), with thanks and acknowledgement to Danske Filminstitut/Per Holst Filmproduktion; p61 **Europa** (4) photography by Rolf Konow, with thanks and acknowledgement to Nordisk Film/Telefilm/Svensk Filmindustri; p61 **Europa** (5), with thanks and acknowledgement to Nordisk Film/Telefilm/Svensk Filmindustri.

Visual material contributed by Steven Soderbergh: p64 **Out of Sight** photography by Merrick Morton, copyright © 2002 by Universal Studios. Courtesy of Universal Studios Publishing Rights, a division of Universal Studios Licensing, Inc. This credit line applies to all stills copyright © 2002 Universal Studios listed herein.; p65 portrait shot from **The Limey** photography by Bob Marshak, with thanks and acknowledgement to Artisan Entertainment; p66 **Erin Brockovich** (1–4) photography by Bob Marshak, copyright © 2002 by Universal Studios; p68 **The Limey** (1, 3) photography by Bob Marshak, with thanks and acknowledgement to Artisan Entertainment; p69 **The Limey** (4–7) photography by Bob Marshak, with thanks and acknowledgement to Artisan Entertainment; p71 **Traffic** (1–5) photography by Bob Marshak, with thanks and acknowledgement to Initial Entertainment Group, Inc.; p72 (1–3); p72 **Traffic** (5, 6) photography by Bob Marshak, with thanks and acknowledgement to Initial Entertainment Group, Inc.; p73 (4); p73 **Traffic** (7, 8) photography by Bob Marshak, with thanks and acknowledgement to Initial Entertainment Group, Inc.; p74 **Out of Sight** (1–4) photography by Merrick Morton, copyright © 2002 by Universal Studios; p74 **Erin Brockovich** (5) photography by Bob Marshak, copyright © 2002 by Universal Studios.

Visual material contributed by Jane Campion: p77 portrait shot from **The Portrait of a Lady** photography by Gerald Jenkins, with thanks and acknowledgement to Polygram Filmed Entertainment; p78 **Holy Smoke** (1–3) photography by Gerald Jenkins, with thanks and acknowledgement to Miramax Films; p79 **Holy Smoke** (5) photography by Gerald Jenkins, with thanks and acknowledgement to Miramax Films; p80 **The Piano** (1–3), with thanks and acknowledgement to CIBY 2000/Jan Chapman Productions; p83 **The Portrait of a Lady** (1), with thanks and acknowledgement to Polygram Filmed Entertainment; p85 **Holy Smoke** photography by Gerald Jenkins, with thanks and acknowledgement to Miramax Films.

Visual material contributed by Ang Lee: p86 **Crouching Tiger, Hidden Dragon** photography by Chan Kam Chuen, with thanks and acknowledgement to Sony Pictures Classics; p87 portrait shot; p89 **Crouching Tiger, Hidden Dragon** (1–10) photography by Chan Kam Chuen, with thanks and acknowledgement to Sony Pictures Classics; p90 **Crouching Tiger, Hidden Dragon** (2–4) photography by Chan Kam Chuen, with thanks and acknowledgement to Sony Pictures Classics; p93 **The Ice Storm** (1, 3) photography by Barry Wetcher, with thanks and acknowledgement to Fox Searchlight; p93 **The Ice Storm** (2) photography by Adger W. Cowans, with thanks and acknowledgement to Fox Searchlight; p93 **The Ice Storm** (4), with thanks and acknowledgement to Fox Searchlight; p94 **Eat Drink Man Woman** (1), with thanks and acknowledgement to the Samuel Goldwin Company; p95 **Ride with the Devil** photography by John Clifford, with thanks and acknowledgement to Good Machine International.

Visual material contributed by Oliver Stone: p97 portrait shot; p100 **Any Given Sunday** (4–6), with thanks and acknowledgement to Warner Bros.; p102 **Nixon** (5–7), with thanks and acknowledgement to Entertainment Films/Cinergi Productions; p103 **Nixon** (8–11), with thanks and acknowledgement to Entertainment Films/Cinergi Productions; p107.

Visual material contributed by Ken Loach: p109 portrait shot; p111 **Bread and Roses** (5, 6) photography by Merrick Morton, with thanks and acknowledgement to Parallax Pictures/Road Movies Filmproduktion/Tornasol Films/Alta Films; p112 **Ladybird Ladybird** (1, 3), with thanks and acknowledgement to UIP/Parallax Pictures; p112 **Ladybird Ladybird** (2) photography by Paul Chedlow, with thanks and acknowledgement to UIP/Parallax Pictures; p115 **My Name is Joe** (1, 2) photography by Joss Barratt, with thanks and acknowledgement to UIP/Parallax Pictures; p116 (4, 5) photography by Merrick Morton.

Visual material contributed by Wim Wenders: p118 **Wings of Desire**, with thanks and acknowledgement to Road Movies Filmproduktion/Argos Films; p119 portrait shot; p120–1 **Wings of Desire** (1–9), with thanks and acknowledgement to Road Movies Filmproduktion/Argos Films; p123 **Faraway, So Close** (1), with thanks and acknowledgement to Road Movies Filmproduktion/Tobis-Filmkunst; p123 **Wings of Desire** (2), with thanks and acknowledgement to Road Movies Filmproduktion/Argos Films; p124 **Faraway, So Close** (1, 2), with thanks and acknowledgement to Road Movies Filmproduktion/Tobis-Filmkunst; p124 **The End of Violence** (3), with thanks and acknowledgement to CIBY 2000/Road Movies Filmproduktion/Kintop Pictures; p127 **The End of Violence** (1), with thanks and acknowledgement to CIBY 2000/Road Movies Filmproduktion/Kintop Pictures; p127 **Until the End of the World** (2), with thanks and acknowledgement to Road Movies Filmproduktion/Argos Films/Mathrab/Village Roadshold Corporation.

Visual material contributed by David Lynch: p131 portrait shot photography by Richard Dumas; p132 **The Elephant Man** (1, 4), with thanks and acknowledgement to Brooksfilms; p137 **Wild at Heart** (1), with thanks and acknowledgement to Propaganda Films/Polygram Filmed Entertainment; p137 **Wild at Heart** (2) photography by Elliot Marks, with thanks and acknowledgement to Propaganda Films/Polygram Filmed Entertainment; p137 **Wild at Heart** (3) photography by Kimberly Wright, with thanks and acknowledgement to Propaganda Films/Polygram Filmed Entertainment; p138 **Twin Peaks: Fire Walk with Me** (3), with thanks and acknowledgement to Guild Film Distribution/Propaganda Films/Lynch/Frost Productions; p140 **Mulholland Drive** (1, 2), with thanks and acknowledgement to Canal +; p140 (3) photography by Suzanne Tenner; p140 **The Straight Story** (5), with thanks and acknowledgement to Canal +/The Picture Factory/Film Four.

Visual material contributed by James Ivory: p142 **The Remains of the Day**, with thanks and acknowledgement to Merchant Ivory Productions; p143 portrait shot; p145 **The Remains of the Day** (1–6), with thanks and acknowledgement to Merchant Ivory Productions; p146 **Mr & Mrs Bridge** (1–3), with thanks and acknowledgement to Cineplex Odeon Films/Merchant Ivory Productions/Halmi; p148 **Howards End** (1–3), with thanks and acknowledgement to Merchant Ivory Productions/Film Four; p149 (4); p149 **A Room with a View** (5, 6), with thanks and acknowledgement to Merchant Ivory Productions; p151 **The Householder** (1–4), with thanks and acknowledgement to Merchant Ivory Productions; p152 **The Golden Bowl** (1–4), with thanks and acknowledgement to Golden Bowl Productions Ltd.; p153 **Bombay Talkie**, with thanks and acknowledgement to Merchant Ivory Productions.

index